A Princess-Cut Diamond

How to reclaim your place of spiritual royalty…..

Cami Deni

Copyright © 2005 by Cami Deni

A Princess-Cut Diamond
by Cami Deni

Printed in the United States of America

ISBN 1-59781-236-6

All rights reserved solely by the author. The author guarantees all contents are original and do not infringe upon the legal rights of any other person or work. No part of this book may be reproduced in any form without the permission of the author. The views expressed in this book are not necessarily those of the publisher.

Unless otherwise indicated, Bible quotations are taken from the New King James Version. Copyright © 1995 by Zondervan.

www.xulonpress.com

Acknowledgements

*H*umbled by the awesomeness and coolness of God, I give all honor and praise to him for all He is to me; all He has done for me and all He chooses to do with and through me.

I want to start by acknowledging my parents, Rev and Mrs. Harold M. Stephens Sr. All I am in God started with the two of you. In Memory of Grandma Belle and to My Grandma Gert, who didn't live to see her desire of publishing a book, come to past.

To my last surviving grandparent "Nanny", there is no one quite like you.

To my siblings LeVonne, Joe and Maceo…the ones who really know me and still think I'm pretty decent. I am excited to see what God will do next with each of you. To Gene, Crystal and Janis if we had to choose to add a few more to the pot they would be just like you guys. To my nephew and niece brigade- Kevin, Stefon, Cameron, Jay-Jay, Joshua, Jade, Dessi Jo (Destiny), and Jorell. Auntie loves ya.

To my Bishop and Spiritual Parents, Bishop Jack C. Wallace and Pastor Gael Wallace. I praise God for you and all you have taught me. Thank you for the seeds you've sown, the example you *set and the sacrifices you make. This book will reach many who like me had no idea who they were in God. Your ministry will reach even further out to them through me. The Kingdom is wiser because of you. To my spiritual brother and Sunday school teacher Elder Ben Gibert and his wife Minister Charisse Gibert. Hanging around you has taught me not to be a wimpy whiny girl ....'cause sometimes "ya' just gotta get nasty !!!"*

To Detroit World Outreach, for being the best at looking like heaven on earth. There is something incredible about worshipping God with you. This is just my lil' part at seeking and saving that which is lost, destroying the works of the devil and living the abundant life !!

To the Jamerson Family, To Cheryl and the Gransdens crew, To Pastors Robb& Sherry Stancer and the Drama Ministry. To Pastor Wes Chubb and the Baddest media crew on the planet, To Purity with Purpose, to Pastor Matt, To Elder Steve and to Cynthia, my prayer shield, thank you, I am so glad you have made it to the other side to help me across! To my new nieces, Taye and Joya~Auntie loves her babies. To Elder Marvin and Bridget (my twin).

To Love, Love and Pitts. I have no idea what to put here that could express what you guys mean to me, so I'll try again in the next book. To Angela, Dreenie, Queen Jackie, Auntie Bonnie, Rev. Bernard, Rev. Rodney, G-Ma Carol, my godparents-Soloman Irvin and James Ella Irvin, Wilma Joyce and David.

To Holy Hope and Messiah, Mr. Reese, and Mr. and Mrs. Javan Turnbough

Lastly, I want to thank and acknowledge my children, Stevan, Jerica, Bryan, Jaivon and Jordan. Thank you all for sharing your mommy with this book. Especially to you Jordan for not touching the computer buttons when you were tempted to. You guys are my joy. I am encouraged to be better and do great things because of all I want for you. Remember, "Many of life's failures are from people who didn't realize how close they were to success when they gave up". Mommy loves you guys.

Dedication

To John-

    Simply put, this book would literally not exist without you, your diligence and your love for me. Thank you for lifting me up when I couldn't reach. Thank you making me type, when I would have rather cried. Thank you for seeing in faith when my vision was clouded in fear. Thank you for making up the difference when I fell short. Thank you for not only calling me a princess, but for treating me like one and making me like it! You are a prince and the very righteousness of God through Christ is displayed no better than through your life and the way you give of your heart to me. Every good and perfect gift comes from God, and you John are good and perfect for me. I thank God for you.
    I am everything I am today, because you love me.

Camille

Table of Contents

1. As a Woman Thinketh 13
2. Princess Boot Camp 21
3. The Lost Princess 31
4. State your Name, Rank and Kingdom 41
5. She Shoots, She Scores 51
6. Get Nanny's Purse 67
7. The Big Fat Princess 81
8. Tattered Presents and Broken Gifts 87
9. The Unaware Advantage 95

CHAPTER ONE

As a Woman Thinketh...

My name is 'Camille" which means virginal, unblemished character, pure and noble. My life says: children born out of wedlock, a failed marriage, dysfunctional relationships, cycles of poverty and misfortune, loss of possessions, reputation and esteem. Have you ever felt that this "Christianity thing" just wasn't going to work out for you? You have fallen too many times. Your clothes are ripped, your face is dirty, and you have bruises that won't heal and memories that won't fade. That unplanned pregnancy still haunts you. You can still see the hand of the man that hit you and feel his punch in your stomach. Your mind goes back to those nights when your heart said no, but there you were almost on the outside looking in seeing yourself fall prey to sexual sin. Your best girlfriend dies at an early age. Your children are disobedient and rebellious.

You think of the day you lost your job, your car, or your husband. Or the day you saw your home and possessions burn up in a fire. You feel tired as you see the mound of debt rise as high as your needs. You cry silently and alone as your children go to bed still hungry from not having enough to eat. You are so busy on a day to day basis, fighting crisis after crisis that it takes its toll on your relationships and lifestyle. You come off as mean, angry, cantankerous, snappy and standoffish when in fact you are just tired, worn out and exhausted from being the player, coach, fan,

A Princess-Cut Diamond

trainer and referee in the plays of your life.

But Sunday after Sunday you show up in church, dress pressed, shoes shined with a smile plastered on your face, Bible under your arm and tithes in your hand. Yet, in your head, you hear the thoughts you dare not say....

"God, if I don't hear from you today, I don't think I will live through this week"

"I am on the verge of crying and I am sick of crying"

" Lord, after what I did, I feel fake, like I don't belong in church"

"Lord I am paying my tithes because you told me to. But you know I don't have enough to make it though the week. You have got to do something."

"Does anybody around me notice that I am hurting"?

"Lord my children seemed to be afflicted with generational curses and I don't know what to do to stop the cycle"

"Everyone else at this job appears to be doing so well, what's wrong with me"

"Why in the world AM I still here? God, what do you want with me?"

Yet you hear your pastor say that you are God's girl, a daughter of Zion, woman of virtue...a Princess in the Kingdom of the Most High God. You look at your checkbook, your refrigerator, your clothes, your court date, your bills, your job, your issues, your children, your divorce, your marriage, your circumstances and say...I don't think so. I can't be what you are calling me. A princess doesn't live like I do. A princess doesn't have the problems I have or the issues I face. A princess isn't worried, or stressed or out of sorts about anything. She doesn't have to deal with mechanics, credit reports, child support payments, cantankerous bosses, jealous co-workers or overworked teachers. She lives this fairytale life in her palace getting waited on hand and foot...waiting for her Prince charming or training to become Queen of the land. So if I am a Princess, then why is my life the way it is? If I really am a daughter of Zion, does my Daddy care that I don't really know what I am entitled to, nor do I have it? Is it just me? Do I not understand? I am not ruling anything. Everything seems to be in control of me. This can't be the way a "royal" is supposed to live.

I asked the same questions myself. Personally, I had gotten to the end of all understanding. I begin to just exist for the sake of my children; they needed a mom, any mom so I thought. I had no reasoning for the disasters in my life, and the slimy pit was too deep, too dark and too familiar to leave. I stopped wondering why. I stopped caring why. I just wanted life, as I knew it to be over with. My mind was a barrage of bad memories and recollections of stupid mistakes and gross errors in judgment. I trusted no one. Folks had proven themselves to be fake and when the "grits hit the fan" they were all about themselves. People I thought I could count on folded under the pressure of their own weaknesses and insecurities. God didn't have much credibility with me. From my vantage point, He had let me down continuously. I didn't trust Him. I felt I couldn't afford to, just in case He didn't come through and I was left on my own, again. I felt uncovered and alone.

Men came, Men went. I experienced dating-relationships with men who were an odd combination. Some were selfish, A.D.D, self-centered, cheaters, ministers, "cheating ministers", abusive, egotistical, whiny, drug addicted, silly, broke and mean. I settled for mediocre over and over again. I wanted to know love and be loved in return, but everyone appeared to have an ulterior motive to being involved with me or I changed who I was to be with them. As far as other areas of my life, I had all of this training, potential and talent but no direction. I felt as if God could not use me, as a matter of fact I felt used up. I had no meaning to my life, no purpose.

I continued in this crazy existence when things slowly started changing. The things my Bishop was pounding into my head every Sunday about who I really was in God, started to take root. My Sunday school teacher started planting seeds of practical faith and how to live a successful life in Christ. The bricks of my foundation from my church as a little girl started to strengthen again and though still a little shaky, I begin to believe that I could make it….at least survive anyway. I started truly praying again. I began studying the Word like I was supposed to. Though, still dealing with issues, still juggling trial after trial, still weeding out "knucklehead" men, I was handling things a little better. Then, God sent John. Just great, I thought.... another guy, another man who will come and go. Not so, his unique situation tried my patience and temperament. However, his uncanny ability to see past the mask and through to the core of me, was God sent and perfect in timing. It had been prophesied before that he was coming (that's another story, for another book). He would not let me settle for just existing. He helped me back on my feet and held me there until I could stand on my own. He spoke life back into me and I believed him. I thought, maybe I could still write a book. Maybe I could break the cycle of poverty in my life. Maybe I could build a legacy for my children. Maybe I could travel all the places I wanted to go, and buy all the cool things I wanted to have for the kids and me. However, there was one issue. One **BIG** issue as far as I was concerned.

My past. All of that baggage was heavy. It was just as much a part of me as John was. Between the two of us, we had more baggage than a major airline. I couldn't let it go. I didn't know how. I wasn't sure how God originally intended my life to be, so I didn't know how to get it back on track. One thing for sure, is that I had jacked it up royally, or so I thought. I knew that I was at a critical juncture in my life. I felt as if I was on a cliff and one step in the wrong direction could be the end.

I took a course at my church called Purity with Purpose. Encouraged by the testimony of others who had taken the course, I felt that it was the right time for me to commit to finally enrolling. It was a 12-week, intense, discipleship course. The class was designed to help you discover what your name means, what your God given life purpose is, how to relinquish soul ties from your past, how to develop spiritual disciplines and much more. At the end of the course, we had a graduation ceremony and there were ministers there that were specifically anointed to speak a prophetic word in your life. The things they spoke I will never forget. One thing stood out though that since then caused me to question my current mindset at the time about who I was and who God saw me to be. The prophetess said that when she saw me that she saw me in the spirit in a mound of dirt. She asked God to reveal why she was seeing this and the spirit asked to her to dig in the dirt. She saw a diamond. It was dirty, grimy and muddy but a diamond nonetheless. She said that the mud and dirt was representative of the past, what I had went through, what I was believing about myself, but regardless of that in God's eyes I was still valuable. I was a diamond.

This revelation coupled with the confirming words of my Bishop, my Sunday School Teacher and John...

"You are an awesome spirit being with infinite potential"

"You are the head and not the tail"

"You are above only, and not beneath"

"You are a Daughter of Abraham and heir to the promises of God"

"You are a Princess..."

I started thinking just like you. Either they are lying...it's just a bunch of preacher hype or I am missing something. How in the world am I to be what they are calling me. I needed an example, a guide, or a handbook. I read every woman's related book I could find. I read about wise women, godly women, loosed women, virtuous women, women that were going through, women on the other side of through, women in business, women who stayed at home, single moms, divorced women, women in ministry, women with hope, women without hope. Though awesome resources, I couldn't find exactly what I was looking for. Why does God expect me to believe that I am privileged, when I am in lack? It came to me while I was writing another book, that a Princess is who she is because of her relationship to the King of Kings. It has nothing to do with what she currently has or doesn't have. Regardless to what she has done, been through or how she looks ~it does not negate the fact that because of who her Daddy is, she is a joint heir to the throne. My Sunday school teacher taught course on the benefits of a covenant relationship. Being a daughter of Abraham has its benefits. God promised Abraham certain blessings that would flow to his seed. We are considered sons (daughters) of Abraham because of our relationship with Jesus Christ (Galatians 3:14). Abraham's actual son of promise was Isaac. So, what's it like to be a son of Abraham? Let's look at some of the blessings of Isaac's life. First of all he was born to Abraham, the richest man in the land. He was born into wealth. He never suffered lack or lived in poverty. Secondly, Isaac sowed seed and received a one hundred fold return (Genesis 26). So for every seed he planted, his crop was one hundred times bigger than what was put in the ground. Third, Isaac re-dug the wells that were stopped up by the Philistines. Those wells were his father Abraham's, so being Abraham's son, Isaac felt a right to the water that was being stifled in those wells. Lastly, Abimelech, who was Isaac's enemy, came to him to make a covenant after recognizing the power of God operating in Isaac life. The Bible says in Galatians 4:28 "Now we brethren as Isaac was are the children of promise." As a daughter of promise what should you expect?

You were born-again as a rich heiress. You should never lack resources to live an abundant life.

Whatever you sow has the power to reap at least one hundred fold.

Your relationship with God empowers you to re-dig the wells that the enemy may have stifled in your parents or grandparents. Dreams that have died, you can resurface because of who you are.

Your enemies-"**The haters**" will recognize the power of God operating in your life and want to bless you because of the respect they have for your anointing.

I shared that reminder to tell you that as heirs in the natural, we know that we do not gain any stored inheritance until someone dies. In the spiritual realm, Princess, please realize that everything that God has promised you is yours. You are entitled to your inheritance NOW because not only did Jesus die, but he also resurrected with all the power you need in his hands.

This book will take you through the some my personal experiences positive and negative and what I learned in the princess in training process. Also, as you relive some painful experiences with me, I pray that you will no longer feel alone in your struggle. I pray that the enemy can no longer have you to believe that only YOU have gone through this and that if you are still dealing with *"that"* then you can't possibly be what God has called you to be. We are saved. We may be bruised, battered, tired and dirty, but we are God's girls and I believe that if we allow him to do some digging through the dirt, He will reveal the **Princess-Cut Diamond** in both of us. After a little training, and some mind renewal, you will place your crown back on your head, brush off your jeans and get back to ruling the kingdom God has given you.

Reflection and Application

1. How do you view yourself? Do you think you are smart, strong, weak, emotional, cautious, tenacious, jealous, fearful? List all the characteristics that would adequately describe you whether you feel they are positive or negative.

2. What are some names you have been called by yourself (ex. Hitting yourself in the head and saying "I'm stupid") or by others. Include nicknames, names you were teased with, reputation labels (like "fast", loose, easy, mean, tomboy etc..)

3. Which of these characteristics, labels or names are masks for something else? Ex. You are viewed as mean when actually you are just snappy or sarcastic to hide what you really think or feel. Which of these names did you end up living up to, although they weren't positive or true? Which ones do you need to release and dismiss from your thought life?

4. In your studies, attempt to find your attributes in characters in scripture. For example if you listed jealousy as a characteristic, study King Saul and learn what his jealousy of David ultimately cost him. If you listed a physical characteristic (i.e. fat, skinny, acne etc..) you can look at the Prophet Elisha (2 Kings) who was teased because he was bald.

5. Learn Habbakuk 2:3 and exercise patience through reading the rest of this book. Your revelation will come.

Hab 2:3 "For the revelation awaits an appointed time, It will speak of the end and will prove not false. Though it tarry wait for it, for it will certainly come and will not delay" NKJV

CHAPTER TWO

Princess Boot Camp

A movie that came out a few years ago titled "Enough" depicts accurately the emotional rollercoaster and tenacity required to overcome fear and fight back against a tormenting enemy. Let's look at the plot and relate it to our own situation. The character in this movie had marital issues, but any major problem can be substituted here.

The desertion of a father, the death of a mother, a job as a waitress...Not exactly the ideal "happily ever after" life that Slim envisioned for herself. She lived day in and day out in a mediocre existence that became her contentment but not her dream. Secretly she always wanted to be happy, secure, loved and have a man in her life that would take care of her and treat her like a Princess.

Mitch, a sleek, sneaky con artist was lurking about ready to prey on Slim's insecurities. He watched her at the diner where she worked, when she wasn't looking. He noticed her strength and learned that it was just a façade of the scared little girl within her. With the help of his college buddy, he planned the perfect ploy to reel her into him. At just the right moment and with just the right deception, He was able to dupe her into thinking that he was her knight in shining armor.

Before long Slim and Mitch were happily married and had a daughter. Mitch, being very wealthy and prominent in the community gave Slim all that she ever dreamed of. The perfect house, luxury cars, designer clothes, credit cards, affluent schools, unending resources and influence were all at Slim's disposal. She was happy. She was safe. He promised to protect her. He promised to always provide for her. She was at peace. Her life was perfect. But a startling deception that finally surfaced was just the beginning to the rapid unraveling of her perfect little world. Slim could of chosen to acquiesce to her circumstances. She could have picked to settle for what was happening to her. For a while she did just that. She believed that she deserved what was happening to her. She was paralyzed in fear. She couldn't go forward and she couldn't go backward. She buckled under the pressure until finally she had had ENOUGH.

I was just going about my everyday life, growing stronger spiritually, and doing what I was "supposed" to be doing. I was getting more involved at my church home. I was making an impact in the kingdom. I had begun to learn some of the enemies lies that I had been taught. Then out of nowhere WHAM, I'm flat on my back. But how did the enemy still catch me off guard? I remember my thoughts so vividly... *How did "this" knock me to the floor? Lord, I was so happy. I never would have thought that "this" would have happened to me........*

There is a mentality that comes with being trapped. It's one of helplessness, low self -esteem or just the feeling of being stuck. You can't move forward or backward. You can't go up and it appears you can't go any further down. **You are paralyzed**. How do you get out of the trap? You make a step, a declaration; you find your "promise" about your situation in the word and declare the truth...that's sounds good. That's sure to get you out of your mess. You search for formulas, 10 steps to...7 ways to...nothing seems to work. You write your issue on a piece of paper and take to the altar. You think that will surely end it. You fast for a meal or two. You sow financial seeds. You sacrifice your time for ministry and make an effort to help others even though you're in pain. But at the end of the day...When your head hits the pillow, sleep evades you and your issues snuggle next to you under your warm blankets. Now what? It's not leaving! It's not moving! "I can't keep going on like this, I need to just forget about it ".

Let's look back at Slim's situation. Mitch's pager beeps while he is in the shower. Slim hears it on the kitchen counter and seizes the opportunity to confirm her suspicions. She looked at it and it was a two-digit number, obviously a code. Slim grabs Mitch's cell phone, searches for that code and presses dial. A woman with an accent answers rather provocatively since she assumed it was Mitch returning her call. The woman, startled when she heard Slim's voice, confirmed the unthinkable. Mitch had been having an affair. Anger, rage, hurt, and disbelief were the array of Slim's emotions. She didn't know whether to break something or cry. When Mitch emerged from the shower, Slim confronted him with her newfound revelation. He hemmed and hawed, but eventually in all of his arrogance, admitted it. He stated it actually like it was the norm. The impression that he gave Slim was that because of what he had done for her, that she should just accept this and deal with it. **BAMN!!!** Not only was Slim humiliated and angry by what she found out, she was belittled and her esteem crushed by being made to feel that she should just be resigned that her husband had two women and that was that. She felt like someone had just kicked her in the stomach. This information and Mitch's attitude left her reeling. This first hit had her stumbling and she had no idea what to do next.

Beloved, that is where some of you are right now. You experienced a "hit"~ something unexpected and unforeseen. It didn't kill you, but you have lost your footing and are unsure what to do or say next. Maybe it was something on the job like sexual harassment, layoff or demotion. Perhaps you and your spouse have been having communication problems or even threatened a separation. It could be your teenager who won't submit to you or to God, he is doing poorly in school or she is running with the wrong crowd. It could be an injury, a court date, a bad report card, or a shut-off notice, overwhelming financial difficulties, issues with siblings, parents or friends…All you know is you are off kilter.

It's a "first hit" situation. More than likely, you've been through something like this before. It hurts, but in all honesty you know you can get through it. A little prayer, a little patience and some faith in what God's Word says and you will begin to see the dawn in your situation. First hits are common and can floor you. In a boxing match everybody expects the boxers to get hit at least ONCE. It's the nature of the game. First hits can also cause you to deal with a small bout of doubt and unbelief. When you can't make sense out of what is happening and you don't see God, your mind will entertain thoughts that God is faithful or that his promises aren't true.

The enemy knows this as well. He's also knows what you have already overcome. In Slim's case, she's been alone before. She'd been broke before. She could handle this. So, Mitch needed to make sure that Slim didn't or couldn't do anything to cause him to lose the upper hand in this situation.

When she confronts him about his infidelity, Mitch basically tells her that not only should she accept his adultery but also that he basically owns her. When Slim stands up for herself, he physically beats her and warns her never to leave him.

As soon as she can, Slim grabs her daughter and runs away. It doesn't take long for Mitch to catch up with her. Before he can hurt her she manages to get away. With his connections to the police department and vast resources Mitch is able to chase his wife and find her using his goons to intimidate anybody that comes in his way. But every time he gets close to grabbing her, Slim gets away.

After several close calls, Slim decides to stop running away and start fighting back. She cuts her hair and takes martial arts lessons as she plans her counterattack.

The situation has escalated now and so have the stakes. It's what we call in church circles "new levels-new devils". At first Mitch's motive was to scare Slim into submission. He wanted to demean her enough to suck the life out of her. But then when she went to a wise older man and told him about her situation, he told her the truth. Mitch was trying to kill her. Now her life was at risk. Slim could have decided to just lie there and let him come. She could have decided to keep running. But when she understood and accepted that her very life depended on what she did next, she decided what all of you must decide to do-TO FIGHT BACK!

Recently, there have been some things in your life that have knocked you out cold. For you, it's more than the bills. It's more than your kids acting up. It's more than not having a "prospect" for marriage. You have had a man mistreat you, lie to you and cheat on you in your face. He may have pretended to be your "knight', but when it all came out in the wash, he was a "Knight mare". Your son is on drugs and hanging with the wrong crowd. Your daughter is pregnant. You have made some mistakes that have cost you big and now its payday. The court trial is set. The divorce is final. The lab test came back positive. School starts soon and you have no tuition. Your mother, brother, or husband still isn't saved. Your "friends" have spread awful rumors about you and true or untrue-they hurt. Your checkbook is not just low, it's empty and you have no idea whatsoever what to do with that eviction notice taped to your door. Your credit is horrendous. Your car is down and your job is on shaky ground.

What do you do now? You are hurt, in pain, broken, confused and you can't seem to get out of this cycle. The enemy is standing over you counting....10, 9, 8, ...are you down for the count? Can you get back up after all you have been through? You've have never hurt like this before. This is the worse it's ever been. It doesn't seem possible that this is even happening to you. You think you have no fight left. You're sick of crying and you're tired. You are afraid. You feel used and useless.

You need a plan. Slim was strategic in her counterattack. She just didn't go over Mitch's house and hit him back. The first thing she did was got her daughter to safety over a friend's house. Secondly, she hired a trainer. Third, she strengthened her body through diet and exercise but more importantly, she re-learned who she was and what she could do. Lastly she laid out a plan to defeat Mitch and executed it.

This guide will take you through a spiritual boot camp experience. I feel you should spend at least a month in this book. It won't take you that long to read it, but to really digest the ideology and to begin to work some principles; I recommend you take your time. Read it and re-read it. It is my goal eventually to sponsor conferences and seminars where we can come together and "workout". Look for my upcoming 90-day devotional supplement that can help you apply focus points from this book to your everyday experience.

The point is, you have to have a strategic plan to reign as a Princess. You can't just arrive in life unprepared and unlearned and expect the tiara to be waiting. In royal society, a Princess is groomed, tutored and trained for years sometimes before she can assume her role. It's not a pretty, nor popular process but you can do it. We will do it! We can DO all things through Christ, which strengthens us. I emphasize the "DO" because it will require WORK. You will put in some sweat equity sister girl. It did not take you a week to get in this mess...and it will take more than a week to get out. But when is a better time to start the process..now or later?

Get your "daughter" to safety.

You're saying... wait, I don't have a daughter or I don't want to send my child away!! You don't have to. For this purpose, "daughter" will represent anything or anyone you are responsible for. During this process, you do want to make sure that you are still meeting the basic needs of your husband and /or children. This also applies if you are taking care of a parent or other loved one. During the next month or so, you may need to call in some support. Tell a friend you can trust to be praying with you as you read this book. Also mention to her that you may need help from time to time around the house and with your errands. If you are the President or Ministry leader in some area, you may need to ask the vice president to give you some extra support during this time so you can focus your attention on your strategy. If you are on any non-essential community oriented committees, you may want to consider a short leave of absence while you take the time to re-evaluate your line of attack.

Hire a Trainer

You have taken care of part of this. I, through this book will be your personal trainer. Make no mistake about it though; you **have** to surround yourself with the RIGHT people. Find women who are where you'd like to be, or like you want to be and learn from them, serve them as armor bearers if you can. Ask to do a brief interview with them. Find out what they have had to overcome to get where they are. It will do no good to go through this exercise, learn your scriptures, work through your reflection and application lessons to only go hang out with people who are speaking defeat, doubt and unbelief. I will also tell you that at the gym, a trainer makes you push a little harder than you would if you if you were working out alone. He will coax you into doing one more set of lifting weights or one more lap around the track. Some of these instructions may push you a little further than you would go on your own and that's GREAT!! That's my purpose. Slim's trainer taught her three very important principles. 1. He made her to know her own strength. 2. He taught her to fight blindfolded. 3. He taught her how to fight when she was flat on her back.

You will learn that the joy of the Lord is your strength. Through working through some of your hindrances and misconceptions about who you are you will find that you have more power at your disposal than you thought. You will also learn to fight when you can't see. When you don't know how God is going to work it out, you have to still stand for the kingdom that God has entrusted to you. When the enemy through persecutions, trials, tribulations and pain knocks you down you will still swing even lying flat on your back! Your kingdom is worth the training. It's worth the fight.

Strengthen your body through diet and exercise.

This is both physically and spiritually. You must know the importance of being physically fit. We won't cover a lot of ground in this area, but your body is the temple of the Holy Spirit. You should care what it looks like and what you put in it and on it. God can use your toned abs or healthy eating as a bait to draw someone into a conversation with you. There is someone at the gym that may need that flyer from your church. Someone you meet while jogging could change your life forever. God can use anything we have to bring him glory, if we submit it to him. For introductory purposes, let me just implore you to see your doctor and begin an exercise program. Try nothing too major or outlandish. Just try an hour on a treadmill while you watch your favorite program or listen to a book on tape. "Fast" walk in the mall early on the weekend. Anything physical that you can do to get you up and moving will be a great start. Start eating right. Not necessarily diet, just eat what you are supposed to eat. Fruits, vegetables, water, protein etc… are essential. Take a daily vitamin. The added physical activity will give you more energy, if you can believe that. You will usually feel better and have a clearer mind if you take the time to stretch, walk, jog, or lift weights. You may have a little soreness the next day, but if you stick with it eventually your flesh will submit to having to physically performing for you. You flesh will be under subjection and know that it will have no cupcakes, chips, or soda as a main meal anymore. Your temple is precious and should be revered as such.

Spiritually speaking, you have to eat the "Word". Your diet will consist of eating the scriptures I have given you to memorize. You should also read the stories of the biblical examples I have given you. Daily read and meditate on the Word of God. Take notes on what you read and highlight anything that that stands out to you. Pray and ask the Spirit of God to reveal what he would have you to know. Be mindful of what your Pastor is preaching on, and what subjects your church Bible study is focusing on. Get supplemental material (books, articles, and other biblical references) that magnifies the subject you are being taught. Spiritual exercise is DOING what you are taught here. As I stated before you will have to DO some work. The Word doesn't work until you do it. Deliverance for many people in the Word came after an act of faith on their part. Naaman had to dip in a dirty body of water 7 times for his healing. The blind man had mud put on his eyelids before he could see. The women with an issue of blood had to touch the hem of Christ's garment, before she was made whole. You are going to have to step out there and work the Word and watch the Word work. That business you want to start will not start unless you take the chance. That book you want to write will never get published until you put the pen to the paper. The weight you want to lose won't come off with out changing your eating habits. The relationship you want to improve won't happen without your communication and cooperation. Be ready to EXERCISE your faith. Your spiritual muscle will get a workout. You will have some sore days. But your flesh will eventually submit and these disciplines will become a part of your new norm.

Boot Camp, even in the military is about discipline. They press you to get up early in the morning. Have your shoes shined a certain way and your hair cut in a uniformed matter. Be able to do this many sit ups, this many pull ups, and be able to run a mile in under this time. All of these directives are for the specific purpose of promoting discipline and endurance. My goal is to develop you to get to the point that after this book and beyond you will have the stamina, fortitude and resilience to outlast the enemy and defeat him.

Reflection and Application

1. What areas in your life do you feel trapped? How did you get in that position?

2. What's going on in your life that you could use help with, or reprieve from?

3. Physically speaking are you in good shape? What small steps can you make to improve your fitness and health? When was the last time you went to the doctor FOR YOURSELF?

4. What issue has you flat on your back? Are you willing to do whatever is takes to get back up again?

CHAPTER THREE

The Lost Princess

Anastasia is a fabled Russian princess that I had never heard about until I watched the movie with my daughter, Jordan. It is believed, as indicated by the movie, that when this Romanov princess was very young, an enemy of their kingdom separated her from her father and other siblings, named Rasputin. Though her father and siblings were all killed, Anastasia's grandmother always believed that she was still alive somewhere. Little did she know that Anastasia had been found on the streets, and was being brought up in orphanage in another country. Slowly but surely as years went on, she began to forget whom she was. The princess lived beneath her privilege. Remember, she didn't remember who she was; therefore know one around her treated her with special respect as they would a royal. They assumed that she was like everyone else. Anya (which is what the child grew up calling herself, as that was all she could remember of her name) was approaching the age of 18 and could then leave the orphanage and strike out on her own. She had no idea who she was, who she belonged to, or that she was royalty. She grew up being taught that she was as an orphan with no family and nothing to call her own.

However, when she had decided to leave, the mistress of the house commented how glad she was to see her go. She stated that Anya always acted snooty like she was "somebody". Anya always took leadership and delegated authority liked she was in charge…like she was "royalty". Anya's actions confirmed what she knew, but could not prove-that she was in fact somebody. She knew in her heart that she belonged to someone and that she had a family. She felt she was not an orphan left alone with nothing. Regardless of the small hard bed she slept in, the watery soup she had to eat everyday, and the scruffy, torn clothes on her back, she felt that she was rich, she just needed to understand where these feelings came from and why.

Anya eventually set out to find her family, but instead ran into a guy, Dimitri, who wanted to teach her How to be Princess. What Anya didn't know was that her grandmother, The Duchess, had put out a decree across the land to find Anastasia. She would give a hefty reward to the person that found her granddaughter. Dimitri wanted to use Anya to trick the Duchess into thinking that she was in fact Anastasia. Dimitri nor Anya knew that Anya really **was** the Lost Crown Princess of Russia. Dimitri, having spent most of his life in the palace as a little boy, knew all about Anastasia, what she liked, her demeanor, her history and how royals acted. He began to teach Anya, how to eat, how to walk, how to talk, what to wear, her royal history, her family tree, how to ride a horse, and he showed her the finer things in life she should expect and recognize as a royal. Then it happened, somewhere in the middle of those training sessions, Anya started remembering things Dimitri didn't teach her. She started acting like a royal. She began expecting the best for herself. She began to hold her head up. She started walking different, talking different. She started to come to grips with whom she really was. Dimitri turned out to be a godsend. He put her on the road to finding her destiny. Let's look at how Anastasia parallels to our lives and the lies the enemy would have us to believe.

Anastasia. Her very name was a clue to her destiny. It means, "She will rise again". Anastasia had forgotten her name. She became what people called her, "Anya". When Dimitri started speaking "Anastasia" back into her mind, she had to rise again. It was the very essence of who she was. What does your name mean? What are you calling yourself? Can you hear me calling you…who you really are?

She was separated from her inheritance because of a tragedy brought on by her dad's enemy. Our Daddy has an enemy also. Satan wants to continue to separate you from all you have in the abundant life Christ died for.

After being away and detached from who she was she eventually forgot who she was-and began to live below her privilege. If you are in a church that doesn't affirms and reaffirms who you are in God, you will forget. If you hang around girlfriends that call each other all kinds of derogatory, slang names, you will forget. If you don't constantly confess and know within yourself that you are the righteousness of God in Christ, you will forget and start to live beneath the intent God has designed for your life.

Even when she wasn't sure why, something within her would stir up...and she would began to act like who she was until reality set back in. Every once in awhile, you get a sampling of the "blessed life". You are living godly, studying like you are supposed to, paying your tithes, serving in ministry, speaking and walking in faith, fasting and praying. Things are happening for you. You get a new job. Your child gets a good progress report. You meet a nice guy. You were positive that you were on your way. Then, you got denied for the loan. The electric bill came in the mail. The car needs a new transmission and you got a call from the doctor's office stating you need an appointment a.s.a.p. You immediately stop speaking faith and start panicking. You accept what you see as fact instead of continuing to believe what you know as truth.

She didn't remember who she was; therefore no one around her treated her with special respect as they would a royal. They assumed that she was like everyone else. When you don't know who you are, and whose you are, you conform your character to those around you. You act like they act. You say what they say. You do things you thought you would never do, because you didn't think any better of yourself and didn't think that anybody cared. You placed no value or self worth on your body, your thoughts, your talents, your abilities, your chastity or your intelligence. You didn't realize your worth and therefore, no one around you did either.

But remember my sister, for this is a key. Once Anya started **acting** like a princess it began coming back to her...who she really was, her identity. You've heard it said that sometimes you have to "fake it til you make it". That's what we call, calling those things that be not, as if they are. Someone who knew what a princess was, had to help her, retrain her, teach her, encourage her, and believe in her. Eventually Anya herself, had to believe.

You know you are living far beneath your privilege. Someone, your pastor, your elder, your teacher, your husband, is telling you who you are. You believe them, but you don't see enough to try to live up to it. If you have enough faith to at least pretend and you can trust the God in me, believe me when I tell you, eventually the role of Princess will fit you like a glove. You had to believe that there was potential for you to become a princess or you would not have picked up this book. Just like Anya had Dimitri to show her her role, you beloved have the spirit of God. In this case, he is using me to remind you, who you are. Have I arrived? Nope. Am I walking total dominance and perfection? Nope. But I can tell you that I am anointed to exhort the women of God to believe who they really are in Christ. I am empowered by the Spirit of God to reveal his intent and his heart to you as his daughter. I know now beyond a shadow of a doubt that I am:

"A awesome spirit being with infinite potential"
"The head and not the tail"
"Above only, and not beneath"
"A Daughter of Abraham and heir to the promises of God"
"I am a Princess in the Kingdom of the Most High God..."

When this training is over, my prayer is that the spirit of God will began to reveal himself to you in ways unimaginable before. I pray that you like the little lost princess will begin to remember, what circumstances, pain, tears, persecution and trials have caused you to forget. You my sister are a royal priesthood and you have a Kingdom to oversee. You **will** become that which you say. Feelings, emotions, what you see, and anything anyone has said that doesn't line up with the Word of God, has no bearing or power over who you are. You will develop into what you confess to be through your faith in action. You cannot become complacent with your current situation and think that things will get no better. You must not allow your current situation to get you into a "woe is me" mode. You also cannot allow the enemy to trick you into thinking that where you are is where you'll be. Just this high and no further. It gets no better. All lies from the father of lies-satan. I learned that this illusion could floor even the best of us. A few years ago, in a Bible class session, we were having a roundtable discussion and this notion of things getting "no better than they are now" came up.

The room was so full of emotion. Some students were contemplating the trials they were enduring. Others were testifying to the fact of their impending deliverance and faith in God. Church school that day was particularly odd. We weren't discussing the prepared lesson at all. I am not sure how we got on the various subjects, but all of a sudden we were in the throes of just being honest about our Christian walk and our struggles when one testimony placed the heaviest question in the air and possibly changed the lives of all those present. So much so, no one even tried to answer it. It wasn't supposed to be answered then. Just thought about...pondered even. It was dropped like a bomb and tears welled up in every eye. We were thinking the possible not wanting it to be true, but what if it were?

"Elisa", a presuming happily married woman began her life-altering question by sharing some of her heartaches, which came disguised in the form of depression. Keep in mind that on the surface (to all of us in the class), Elisa had it all together. She was the mother of three very sweet children. She had obtained her Master's degree and was married to a very successful businessman and upstanding elder in the church. They lived in one of our metro area suburbs and even had a dog. To us, she had it made. They were as close to the 2 _ kids, a dog and a white picket fence scenario that we had seen. They were living the American dream. Financially, they appeared to be stable (at least more prosperous than the rest of us in class). Spiritually, they seemed to be on track and none of them were dealing with any life threatening illness or issues. So for us to think, or even hear that our cream of the crop was having an issue was a devastating blow to our hope. Elisa told us of her bouts with depression. How she would be fine one day and totally incoherent the next day. She shared with us the toll it took on her children and her husband. She told us that she would have crying spells and would just lash out in anger without warning. There were days that she couldn't speak or function. She couldn't really talk to anyone, and there were many times where she just wanted to give up. She knew the Word of God. She'd study scriptures on the mind, God's healing power, defeating the enemy etc.. She sincerely believed that God could heal her. She knew beyond a shadow of doubt that God could deliver. But would he? Or would this roller coaster of the mind be her lot?

She reflected on a movie she saw starring Jack Nicholson. Jack plays Melvin (a sociopath with many quirks and weird hang-ups) who is seeking therapy to overcome his illnesses. He seems to be making no progress. Nothing has changed, he is not getting better and it is frustrating him. It is at the end of one of these unfruitful trips to the therapist that Melvin (addressing the other patients in the waiting room) asked the same question that Elisa floored us with "what if, this is as good as it gets? "

A hush fell over the room. There wasn't a dry eye in the house and our facilitator, in a struggle to fight back his own tears made every effort to encourage Elisa but he knew, and the class knew that this was a question that was going to haunt our spirits until we addressed it. In all honesty everybody in that class should have been able to answer Elisa's question and confirm it with so much scripture, so many testimonies and so much confidence that her very question would have sounded foolish. However, what gave validity to her statement and to her feelings was her honesty. Most of us felt exactly the same way but are just too afraid to admit it, face it and deal with it. Our classmates talked about it undercover for weeks. We called each other and it would come up. We would see each other in between services and it would come up. I would be caught staring off in service sometimes and I'd have to catch myself from thinking about it. We even called it the "Elisa question". But the bottom line was simple. We all knew and had been taught to an extent about God's ability to heal, deliver, exalt, and his ability that he had given us to produce wealth. We'd studied account after account of what God had done in the past for his children. We had heard testimony upon testimony about what God was doing now.

This wasn't a judgment on the goodness or faithfulness of God. God's word is true period.

The question was, would His promises manifest in our lives? This question also became an awakening to our own motives for serving him. True motives are tough to face. We started thinking, what if this was as good as it got? If I never get healed, my own business, delivered, rich, married, debt free, have a baby, promoted, launched into world wide ministry or anything else we are believing God for and Christ returns can you still say that all was worth it? Every heartache, disappointment, failure, trampled dream, repentance, misunderstanding, broken promise, and battle that you had to endure pales in comparison to the eternal glory that awaits us? Yes, all true. But how did Christ intend for us to live here, on earth? This can't be all there is.

I began to wonder is this all that there is for my children? Is where I am right now the best that life is going to be for me? I begin to feel disappointed and cheated. I started thinking like, hey I've been flamboozled! I feel stuck. Is this all worth it? Well, of course it is.. every old church mother would say. "Just knowing Jesus pays off after while" they would testify. Well, when is after while? I protest! What about all of this money cometh to me NOW stuff? What about being the head and not the tail and above and not beneath? What about things being done on earth just as it is in heaven? What about by his stripes I am healed? Lord, I believe, but help my unbelief.

However, as I grew in the knowledge of the abundant life Christ wants for us to have, I became more confident that this is far from as good as it gets. Oh yes, heaven will be wondrous, far above anything we can imagine. Nonetheless, it's not heaven I am talking about. It's earth. I had to reprogram my thinking to start to believe and confess the life that God wants us to have here. He gave us the power to overcome, sickness, disease, poverty, and depression. He left us with the Holy Spirit to guide us and direct us onto the path that leads to an abundant life. He wants us to fulfill our destiny. He wants and delights in our prosperity. I had to start confessing out of my mouth the way and will of God. Daily, I would say who I was in Christ. I would confess what I was entitled to as a joint heir with

Jesus. Everyday I would do something toward the ministry of writing that God was calling me to. Something changed. My circumstances didn't change. I am in still in debt as I write this. I have family members who are not saved. My kids aren't perfect little angels and job issues abound. However, I changed. My mindset changed. I started expecting change and opportunities. I had something valuable that I had almost lost in the throes of Elisa's question. I had regained hope. Having hope and confidence in an unfailing, righteous, eternal, all -powerful God? Now, that's as good as it gets. Princess, don't lose your hope. No matter how discouraged you get during this process, don't let the enemy fool you. The Bible says all things will work together for the good of them that love the Lord and are the called according to his purpose. So regardless.... it's all good. It may not feel good. It may not look good. But God promised that it will all work out FOR good.

My youngest daughter Jordan, (along with 150 other girls in her school) had the latest, cutest Pink Barbie Book bag. It's state of the art, with zippers, pouches, and it's own water bottle. It's looked so new, clean and organized. Everything is in its place.

I remember her Blue's Clues Book bag from the year before. It too was so cool on the first day. But I also remember around October, an interesting thing happened. The book bag didn't look new anymore. The strap had been ripped. The bottom was dirty from dragging it through the leaves and dirt. The homework folder was ripped in the middle and inside there were broken crayons, pencils and crumbs lining the bottom.

Disgusted with its condition, I decided to just buy her a new one and then my "good sense" kicked in. "Wait a minute," I thought. This is only two months old!! It has to be still salvageable. She can get more use out of this regardless to how it looks now.

I took everything out of it. The ripped papers, the forgotten library books, and undone homework were dumped on the floor along with rocks, hair ribbons, half eaten twinkies and dried up daffodils.

I sewed up strap securely. I turned the bag inside out and put it in the washing machine hoping for the best. I then went through the collage of former contents and decided what stayed and what was thrown away. With a little tape, and a new box of 99 cent crayons we were back in business. Getting the book bag from the dryer was like opening a Christmas present. It looked almost brand new. I repacked it and Jordan barely recognized it the next day. She was ecstatic that it was all fixed up again. She went to school with that first day of class confidence!

I was wondering...........

If I can do that with a 13.99 blue's clues book bag. I wonder what GOD could do with a gal like me.

Am I salvageable? Are my dreams still within reach? Can I actually be cleaned from the inside out? Will I allow God to throw some things in my life away? Can the broken straps of divorce, poverty, depression and guilt be repaired to make me stronger? Can God still use me? Can I be brand new again?

The answer is yes...

Therefore if any man be in Christ he is a new creature... old things are passed away behold all things are become NEW!

Reflection and Application

1. What things or people (past or present) block you from remembering who you are in Christ? Name each of them and declare that particular hindrance removed in Jesus name! In what areas are you being treated as common (relationships, work, family, in the supermarket)? What can you do differently to reflect the light of Christ in your life and reveal who you really are?

2. Because you are God's daughter, His favor is a privilege. What areas in your life do you need God's favor? Begin to speak " I am walking in the favor of God" at least once a day and expect- actually look for the supernatural things (large or small) that God begins to do for you.

3. Do you think that where you are now is as good as it gets? If you are walking in what God has called you to, are you complacent and not seeking to get better, do better or train others? If you are not walking in your destiny, do you know what your destiny is?

Are you taking the steps to find out? (you can put yes here, since you are reading this book !)

4. Renew your mind often "This is not the end. God has more for me to achieve, receive, sow, reap, learn and do!"~ It is not too late, as long as I am here, I have the gift of time!"

Learn Philippians 4:19

I am confident of this very thing, that he who has begun a good work in you shall complete it until the day of Jesus Christ.

CHAPTER FOUR

State your Name, Rank and Kingdom

In order to rule and reign, you must understand what falls under your domain, or what you are responsible for. Your purpose has to be clear and the lines clearly drawn. If you take on more than you are supposed to be able to handle, you may not have the grace to administrate effectively. If you don't own up to the complete calling on your life, you forfeit the blessings that come along with obedience. If you are unclear about your specific purpose in the kingdom, I sincerely recommend Dr. Myles Monroe's book "The Pursuit of Purpose". I also would highly recommend the purity with purpose course (information on how to get that class taught in your church is included in the appendix). Some of you know that you have been called into youth ministry, motherhood, prayer ministry, armor bearer, helpmeet, music ministry, the mission field, etc… Others of us aren't too sure. There are some areas in your kingdom that you can be sure of in the meantime. One issue is, we have allowed time and fear determine what we think we can't be.

I remember a time when I younger when I knew what I wanted to be and then what later made me change my mind. I remember wanting to be a pediatrician. However, I thought college and medical school would be too hard. I wanted to be a newscaster, but didn't think I was pretty enough or could speak well. Even as a high school student the enemy had already began filling me with self-doubt and fear. Then due to an illness one of my best friends died, she was only 14. I was 16 and her death confused me totally. She was awesome. She was talented, so pretty and smart and so much fun. Why would God take someone like her and leave someone like me. I felt bad because I was here and she wasn't. Shonn deserved to live –I thought. God was way wrong for taking her. She had way more to give the world than I did. I underestimated and downgraded my abilities and I underestimated and downgraded God. The same year, I had an English teacher who pushed me beyond measure. I hated her (yes, I have since repented). I thought she was prejudiced. She gave me a D- on a report that I should have gotten at least a B on. I *never* get a low grade in English, what was she thinking? In the end though, I understood and appreciated Shakespearean literature, knew and understood parts of speech that most had never heard of and she made me to become a much better writer. I eventually became the editor of my school newspaper and member of the yearbook staff. I had found my niche'. I thought I could go into journalism and become the editor of my own magazine. I loved writing and I did it well. So, off to college I went. I got sidetracked by stupid mistakes and eventually quit school, had a baby and got married. Being a journalist was out of the question now. Now, I needed a job to help make ends meet. I had a son and he depended on me. Soon after that I had 3 other children and eventually a divorce and all the drama that goes along with that (another book, another time). All of my dreams had been shoved back into the corner. No more time for dreaming. Survival was all that mattered now. "Take care of those kids" is what I told myself daily. They were all that mattered. Eventually years later, I went back to finish school and after three schools, part time courses, classes by video, long distance learning and 15 years later, I graduated. In between there, I managed to win a beauty pageant, have another baby, dump a cheating boyfriend and go through one of the most horrifying, demeaning, heartbreaking experiences I have ever had to encounter. All of these memories came flooding back as I tried to remember, "What happen to my dreams?" How did I get so sidetracked? Or was everything suppose to happen just as it did, so I could be where I am now?

The purity with purpose class helped me to sort this out. We worked diligently at discovering our purpose and understanding all of the "why's" in our lives. The first step was in figuring out what your name actually means. You have to know your name. You must know what God intended when he named you. Now, in the African American culture, be aware that some of our six syllable names were created out of the combining of several names, prefixes, cars, flowers etc…It may require a little more research to get to the root of your name or to find (despite the unique spelling) what the core of your name is.

Without disclosing all of the particulars brought out in class, the in-depth study of names and the purpose behind them was eye opening. Generally speaking, your name defines you and may give you a hint as to God's original intent for your life. Our expectation of how an item, person or animal should look can be derived from its name. For example, if your cat is named "midnight' you would expect to see a dark colored cat. What you are called can identify qualities that are unique to that person. You would expect that a person labeled "teacher" was an instructor of some sort. Lastly, a name can identify a distinctive function for a thing or person as in "tape dispenser". You would expect, (since you know the definition of the two words) that this item would dispense tape. The facilitator goes on to give biblical references and examples explaining the significance of certain names and how their names had a significant impact on the destiny of many biblical people. She also noted how important it was for God to change the name when a current name no longer fit the characteristics or spoke into the providence of a particular individual. (sidebar) If I haven't said it yet, on just what I have learned so far-You have **GOT** to take this course. Just this session alone will give you a whole new perspective of naming your children, what you call people and what people call you.

So now begins the journey of discovering what my name means. In our smaller groups we begin digging through name books and some had searched the internet to find out what their name meant from it's original language. I always thought my name was

French. Actually, it is a common name *used* in France, but at its root it is Latin. The Latin definition for **Camille** (as I stated at the beginning of this book) was virginal, unblemished character, pure and noble. Another definition also added "attendant at religious ceremony". I looked at this definition and although I am glad it didn't say Camille-clown, stupid idiot....to see words like virginal, pure, unblemished made me laugh.

God, "be for real," I thought. You and I both know that I have a house full of kids; I am so far from virginal, pure, clean and unblemished it's ridiculous. I mean I know all the hype phrases and all of the positive confessions but I am thinking this is way off. Further more "noble" that would indicate someone born into an aristocratic family, someone royal, rich, dignified, majestic and stately. Nope, that's not me either....so what's this about?

I was so frustrated. If that was God's intent, well I sat there thinking, so what do I do now? Others were finding out the meaning of their names. It was exciting to see faces light up with revelation, as it appeared that things were made clear right before their eyes. Some were proud of their names and what they meant. When people asked me, I was sort of hesitant to share it. I am sure they thought exactly what I did–"oh reeeeeeeeeally...virginal huh...yeah right." Anyway, our group leader encouraged us to look up our middle names as well. I was thinking, no way. I have had enough revelation for one day. I don't need to hear about anything else I was "supposed" to be. I started praying because I didn't want to be disobedient or bitter.

"God, please give me the courage to just look. I am totally intimidated by this whole thing but it is- what it is. You aren't surprised or shocked. You know my name, you know what it means and you know I have not lived up to the name I have. So, ok here we go."

My middle name is Denise. I looked it up in one book and it refers you to "Dennis" which as *Dionynus* means a greek god or something, but it also said "see Deni". I thought that was odd. When I write I use the pen name "Deni" as my last name. So I went searching for Deni. I flipped to another book, since that one didn't have it..thinking all the while...I wonder what the joke is going to be this time...it will probably say something else that I am not or can't be.... Finally, I found it.

"Deni"- Vindicated

Tears welled up in my eyes as I search further in the description to get synonyms for a clearer understanding. It gave me words like justified, supported, defended and maintained. I sat back in the chair and "meditated" on it. Then I understood what God was trying to teach me. The spirit of God would have this to say....

(I tried to write this as close as I remember it-it was revealed in part and understood in part)

"You were intended to be a person that was innocent in nature, unblemished and virginal in character. Our relationship and your trust in me was supposed to be pure and undefiled from the issues of this world. You have heard it said to you that you have an innocence about you and you have not understood how that can be seen through your mask. But it is the very essence of who you are. You *are* noble and royal as a princess of the most high God. You have felt that you have not lived up to your end of the covenant in many ways. You are right, but you are vindicated. I have defended you against the enemy and you are justified in my eyes"

God's original intent for my life is the very core of my kingdom. The character, the relationship and the nobility he has called me to **by name** will be needed to run the kingdom he intended for me to oversee.

As I stated, we have let time and fear determine what we think we can't be. You may think you are too old to try to change. You may be afraid of moving forward and afraid of going back. You think it's too late to be what you are called to be. It's not. You have still been entrusted to be a ruler. You have a kingdom, no matter what you think.

Your sub-kingdom, with the Kingdom of God being overarching, consists of anything or anyone under your circle of power. Your 1- bedroom apartment, your children, your job, your co-workers, your neighbors and neighborhood, your boyfriend or husband, your dry cleaners, supermarket, mailman all make up your area of influence. Anything in your world, small or as large as it may be, is your "kingdom".

You are responsible to rule and reign over everything God has given you. The issues surrounding your everyday life are subject to God's authority through you. We have identified your kingdom, now let's establish it. On buildings or on charter archives you will see a simple statement that brings to light when that institution came about. It will simply read like the following:

EST 1967

That simple phrase lets you know exactly when something was established and depending what it is on, it let's you know what was established. If you notice though, usually the date is long before the building was made or the first event came about. It became established when the vision was spoken and the faith to make it come to pass became substance. For example, most churches were established when the few people got together and declared this will be a church. You haven't had one church service, and you have no idea who is going to sing, but you became a church.

For you dear princess and your kingdom, write the vision down if you have to. List what areas you have influence over and who is in your circle of responsibility directly or indirectly. List what portion of ministry is under your domain and determine who and what is subject to your authority. Then write down the date and establish it for yourself. You may not have a scepter, tiara or a throne but you are still who God says you are and out the heart confession is made unto your salvation. Declare it out loud today - my kingdom is established in you Lord. Thank you for all you have made me a steward over. Give me wisdom to reign over my responsibilities, circumstances and issues. You have called me by name and I receive your calling in my life.

In establishing your name (knowing who you are) and your kingdom (your area of influence), there is still the small matter of your rank. Your rank determines your status, position, or level of privilege. We have heard what God has called us to be. As mentioned in the previous chapter, we are called to be the head and not the tail. The Bible says we should be the lenders versus the borrowers. Remember, we are the daughters of Abraham and heirs to the promise given to Abraham which was, that those who blessed us shall be blessed and those that curse us shall be cursed. We rank as a joint heir with Jesus Christ. All that is Christ's is ours.

We know the words, but believing it is a different thing. The belief process starts with a decision. The decision to choose to believe is the first step to actually accepting who we are and walking in it. This step is difficult for some because we look at the circumstances instead of looking at the Word. If we can just look past what we are surrounded by, we can be victorious. Two perfect examples of understanding the power of knowing how to dismiss circumstances and view your true rank in God are Peter and Lazarus.

In the familiar account in Matthew, Jesus sent the disciples ahead by boat, while he dealt with the multitude. Peter and the disciples later find themselves alone in the boat in the middle of the storm. Out on the water they see a "ghost", walking on the water that looks like Jesus. Peter tells "the ghost" Lord, if it is you tell me to come to you. Jesus tells Peter to come. Peter steps out and **walks** on the water toward Jesus. He is walking in supernatural favor until he "remembers", Hey, I CAN'T walk on water! Even though he was DOING it and Jesus was right in front of him, the waves and wind made him afraid and he begin to sink. He believed until he remembered the lie that the supernatural was not possible.

Lazarus had been dead three days and his sisters had previously sent for Jesus to come heal him. However, by the time Jesus arrived Lazarus was dead. The Lord asked the sisters to show him where they buried him. Let me pause here to say, that you have to be brave enough to show Jesus where you have buried your hope, your dreams, your ambitions. You have to be willing to search out and reveal where you stopped believing. It is there that your resurrection can take place.

Jesus walks up to the place where they showed him and proclaims that what he is about to do is for the benefit of those who do not believe. Your deliverance Princess is not just for you. It is for the benefit of those who do not believe. There are some people who had written me off as a failure, a statistic, a nobody, who are going to see this book and have a renewed faith in God. They KNOW what God brought me through because they were there. My success is not only for my children, but also for the kids down the street. It's for my co-workers, to encourage them to believe that all things are possible and that God has the power to bring life into a dead situation.

Jesus goes up to the tomb and it is here that I want us to focus our attention. A minister I heard recently brought out an interesting point. Jesus calls out to Lazarus...Lazarus come forth! Notice Lazarus didn't answer back "Lord I can't, I'm dead" ! Lazarus didn't contradict what Jesus had spoken. He was obedient. Lazarus eyes may have opened but remembered they were covered in the grave clothes. Still, when Lazarus heard his name, he still came when he couldn't see his way. His grave clothes bound him and restricted his walking, but Jesus told him to come forth and even struggling to walk, Lazarus submitted to what the Lord said he could do.

Beloved, if God says that you are of a Royal priesthood, don't yell back, but Lord I'm divorced! Just keep on walking. Don't let God say "Stephanie, come forth" and you yell back, God I can't, I don't have enough money. Don't tell God that you have children out of wedlock, or that you are in debt or struggling with an addiction, he knows all that...waddle in your grave clothes if you have to, but come out of the grave. Someone will be there to help you get loose.

I know your relationships, your past, your hurt, your pain, your disappointment and discouragements may make it difficult to walk out, but keep on stepping. If God called you out, you have the power to step! Now THAT's some power that we can use in many areas of our lives. The Power to Step! You know that your job is dead-end. You know that you are capable of more and should be working for yourself. Get your plan together, and when it is time, girl get ta' steppin'. You are in a relationship that is draining you and is sucking the life out of you. You know he isn't living godly. He seeks to blame you for all his shortcomings and make you a co-dependent. Apologize and beg his pardon if you must for hurting his feelings. But then, look that precious brother in the eye and tell him, I love ya with love of the Lord...but I gotta go...then girl straighten up your crown, fix your gown and get ta steppin'. There are people in your life that you need to endow with the power to step! They are all in your space and blocking your path to destiny.

You have a teenager that will not submit to God and won't obey or respect you. Hard as it may be, I been there-done that. You can tell them, bye-bye baby, they too have the power to step! If you have trained them in the way that they should go, when they get old they will not depart from it.

If you have the ear to hear God, you have the power to follow God. Regardless of the storm around you and no matter how rough the seas, You are who God says you are. No matter how bad you may think your issues are, God can still use you. Princess, if you can see Jesus through the rain and through your grave clothes~ your highness YOU have the power to walk on water! Now get ta steppin'!

Reflection and Application

1. Have any of your dreams been placed on the back burner? Which ones and why? Did you change your mind or did you think you couldn't achieve your goals?

2. What does your name mean? Use a baby name book (older publications that you find in the library are usually more accurate) or the internet to do a search. Look up all of your names. Look for synonyms to the words mentioned to describe the name. Pray specifically for the spirit to reveal the deeper meaning of your name(s) and how you can walk in that calling on your life.

3. If you could really view your life as a "sub-kingdom", what would your kingdom be known for? Would it be its generosity, its wisdom, its organization, its talent, its ability to encourage/help others, its honesty, its wealth, its failures....

4. What do you believe the purpose of your life (kingdom) is? Is it to use your talent to minister to others? Is it to become a missionary, a teacher, an entrepreneur? Take into consideration your gifts, talents, abilities, resources, occupation, education, training, desire, confirmed prophecies or words or knowledge, or just your plain gut feeling. This may change as you grow and

develop spiritually, but start by writing your initial thoughts and work towards those.

5. What excuses have you yelled back to God out from your grave? What hinders you from believing that what was dead can be resurrected? Can you trust God enough to come out anyway, believe who you are no matter what storm you are facing now? Confess this "I cannot change what has happened, but I can believe God to change what happens next!"

CHAPTER FIVE

She shoots, She scores!

You have established your subkingdom. You are empowered. You may not feel empowered. You may not appear empowered. However, the title Princess indicates responsibility and work. Yes, God intends for you to run your part in the kingdom. He said in John 1:12 that as many as received him, to them he gave power to become the sons of God. If you weren't going to need power to "become", God would not have needed to make it available. The Amplified version reads ...."He gave the authority (power, privilege, right) to become the children of God. God granted authority, power, privilege and rights for you to operate as a child of the King. It's not meant to be a cakewalk. Kingdom rule is hard work. The title of this chapter is "she shoots, she scores". Shooting and scoring are both offensive moves. Often, we live our lives too much on the defense. Something happens and then we react. Something goes wrong we work to fix it. We get a bad report card and then we seek tutors. The doctor says your blood pressure is high and then you watch your diet. The lights are shut off, and then we call to make arrangements. But in your kingdom, if you work to stay ahead of the game, you can minimize the oncoming issues. If you had seen the progress report, you would have known that your 2nd grader was not doing well in math. If you'd remembered to get the oil changed, you would not be having engine problems now. Princess, you can

A Princess-Cut Diamond

only score points on the offense.

Being an avid World Champion Detroit Pistons fan, I know the importance of defense. We had the best defensive team of the league. But no matter how well the team defended their position, in every game the team with the most points won. You have got to shoot some baskets and not spend all your time putting out the fires of your life. Some baskets you will score, some you won't. This chapter may put you out of your comfort zone or challenge you to be a little different than you are now. But to be something different, you have got to do something different.

I know you have in your head that royals live an easy life, that's only half true. If you study any successful monarchy, you will find people who were about change. They are people who are extremely organized, sacrificial, wise and they have a deep love and commitment to those in their domain. They have people who will fight for them and their vision. They also have people who would like nothing more than to see them dead. They cannot go where they want to go. Wherever they do go, they must have protection. They give of themselves to gain the respect of their constituents. They put their lives in the public eye to develop a reputation of openness and trust. It is true that they live in privilege. Everyday issues aren't normally a concern to them. They usually have someone to clean, mop, cook and take care of the bills. Quiet as it is kept you are supposed to have that also. The Proverbs 31 woman that we have all heard about and use as a role model, had maidservants. She had some money. She owned land and had a business. If you build your kingdom appropriately, you eventually will need an extra pair of hands to help you maintain your home so you can meet the needs of your children, husband and ministry. If you are not there yet, that's ok. In the meantime you have the grace and the power through the Spirit of God to build the foundation of your kingdom.

Running your subkingdom is best described in three parts:

Maintaining your family, home and constituency
Organization of all business affairs
Learning to recognize and destroy enemy camps

Maintaining your family and home

Being a part of a royalty does not dismiss you from having to deal with the responsibility of your children, husband and other family relationships. If you are single, you have relationships with your siblings, parents, friends and significant others that will be affected by your kingdom rule. Your children have to know and understand the importance of how to live as part of a divine lineage. There are things that they cannot do because of who they are connected to. They cannot go certain places, listen to certain things or hang around certain people. They cannot go out in the street unprotected. Ok, they may not have bodyguards, but they do need to understand the significance of the angels that are put in charge of them. They also need to know that they are covered in prayer every time they leave your home. If you are married, your role is different. You have a King in the home that is responsible for the vision and direction of the kingdom. Women are called to be helper to their mate. The word "helpmeet" can be understood clearly with this definition "aid, one who causes pain to cease by rendering assistance". Your help, your assets, your aid, should be so significant that it causes the pains of worry, anxiety, helplessness, inadequacies, and pains of failure to cease from affecting your mate and thus your marriage. If you are married to the mate God has designed for you, you and your destiny are formed and fashioned to fit into his life, his purpose and his vision. Also know that women are to have similar characteristics to the Holy Spirit working in her husband's life. She, like the Holy Spirit should be a comforter, an intercessor, a consolation, and an advocate.

For a more in depth study on how to build your home I recommend, "A Wise Woman Buildeth her House" By Minister Charisse Gibert, Xulon Press. This is a must have for any woman, but especially if you are married, a stay at home mom, or choose to be in the future.

As I stated before, royals willingly give of themselves to gain the respect of their constituents. Their lives remain an open book. Their victories and failures are constantly in the public eye and through that they sometimes develop a reputation of openness, trust and just plain being real people. Putting your business, or rather

A Princess-Cut Diamond

your experiences on front street, is a sacrifice. But again know my sister, your past and what you learned from it, was not just for you. People around you may live in this fear that nobody has gone through "this" but them. The enemy has them isolated and fooled. God will give you opportunities to share your wisdom. Being a princess is as much about ministry as it is about position. Depend on the Spirit of God to give you what to share and how much. God desires that we speak the truth in love. That does not mean **only** when it is the truth about someone else, it means the truth about **you** as well.

For example, a former co-worker named "Carrie" showed me how just a few minutes of sharing and unselfishness could have a lasting impact on lives God places in your path.

I was having one of the worst weeks that I could ever remember. Everything was going wrong. I got the kids off to school and struggled into work. I looked a mess and was on the verge of tears all morning. Carrie must have noticed my demeanor and pulled me to the side a minute. She asked me if I was ok and I said that I would be fine, just having a rough day. After a few minutes, she found someone to cover her position and told me to take a break. She asked me to come downstairs to the parking lot with her. There we found a stoop and sat there as Carrie, who was just a few years older than me, spilled out the Wisdom of Solomon. She said, Camille I have no idea what you are going through and it doesn't matter, but let me tell you this. You can make it. She said it with such conviction, that I was taken off guard. She went on to say that she had been through a lot in life. She had lost a home before, a car, had trouble in marriage, financial difficulties, issues with her son, sometimes thinking she had lost her mind....just a plethora of issues. But she looked me square in the eye and said "I made it- and you can make it, and there is no reason or excuse that can justify why you can't ". Then she told me something that changed my outlook on people forever...She said Camille, if this has to do with people or if someone has hurt you, never forget this...pay absolutely little attention to and quit getting sucked in by what folks with no credibility tell you. You watch what they **DO**. She said, what they tell you is what they want **YOU** to believe; what they **DO** constitutes what **THEY** believe.

That statement changed my whole approach on how I dealt with people. I was able to hear, listen, and respond to the things I was told. But I knew and will always know that the real test is watching what people do. What people say means nothing if keeping their word holds no value to them. I stopped being as gullible and naive and started to weigh the information I received and its source. Another thing I will never forget about that day is how alone I felt before Carrie talked to me. By sharing her experiences and wisdom with me, I felt as if I had someone who really understood what I was going through. She didn't fix anything. She couldn't make all the wrongs right, but she gave me a shoulder and stood high enough on the rock so that even in my storm, I could see her and have hope. Now that's a Princess. The feeling of hope she instilled in me was priceless. Now that's ministry at its finest, but it cost her something. She paid the price by opening up and becoming vulnerable to what I would say and think about the things she was sharing with me. But her openness possibly saved my life. Who knows what could have happened if I had of continued in that downward spiral? There have been other people who have shared their experiences with me, but not often revealing themselves and their own frailty like Carrie did. She made a permanent mark on my life that day and I would never forget the lesson learned. How many marks have you left? Are the people that know you affected positively by you being in their lives? Are you willing to be open and transparent? Often, other people's needs may have to come before your own comfort. The Bible says, If you want to rule and reign with Christ, you will have to suffer with him. His kingdom cost and so does yours.

Organization of all business affairs

Being an administrator by trade, I could write a book just on organization alone. However, for the purposes of this book, the primary thing to understand about your subkingdom is that it must be organized. Managing your life, your children, your marriage, your finances, your job, or your usher board meeting, all must be done with and in the Spirit of Excellence. There is nothing worse than a Princess coming before her people, an hour late, with her crown half on, and looking for her speech under a mound of paper. Simple things speak volumes about your character. What practical things can you do to develop royal character? For my married sisters, don't allow your husband to come home to a messy, dirty home everyday. He shouldn't have to come home from work and step over shoes and newspapers to get in the house. He also should not greet you with your pajamas on and rollers in your hair. I understand you may work also, but Princess, work it out. If you have to, put dinner in the crock-pot before you leave and come home at lunch to at least clean up the living room. Make a place of peace and order for that man and he will always cherish coming home to you. Single gals, you have no excuse to not have your place in order. We have a tendency to be more relaxed because no one is there but us. There are no kids putting crayon marks on the walls. You may not get a whole load of laundry in weeks. You are in training and should God send you a mate your lax days are over. You might as well do for yourself what you would do with someone else. I understand you work and are involved at church but you have to schedule time to clean your home. Keep a clean car, pick up the garbage and keep it washed no matter if it's a Beetle or a Bentley.

Don't gossip or spread rumors. Correct those in love who try to gossip to you. Be on time for your appointments. If you have a rehearsal scheduled, be diligent to get there on time and if you cannot make it, call someone. Build a reputation for being where you are supposed to be. Keep a date book or PDA, and be careful not to over commit yourself. Understand and reestablish your priorities depending on what you are doing. For example, to finish this book, the volunteer work I was doing with a political campaign had to be shelved. In order to spend time with my kids while they are on winter break, I will have to sacrifice a day of work. In order to finish a project at the office, I may have to work on a Saturday. Almost everyday you have to make decisions to handle the priorities in your kingdom. The goal of the ruler is to be diligent to schedule, coordinate and delegate appropriately. If you need some help with your children, find a mother at your church and swap help days. If you need to hold a family meeting to coordinate tennis practice, doctor's appointments, drama rehearsal and what you all will eat for the week, then do it. Even if it is a meeting of one, sit down take a minute to plan your week, your day. Make a list of what you need to get done and the resources required to make it happen.

If you don't have household help yet, began to organize your home yourself. Get your children to organize their bedrooms and drawers. Clean out junk drawers and medicine cabinets. Some of us have more resources than we realize, but when we don't see it (because of clutter) we just buy more and waste time and money. That is not good stewardship. Make sure your husband's things are where he can find them. Get the clothes to the cleaners so his suits are available for him. Take care of his shirts and make sure the cabinets are stacked with his favorites (provided that they are good for him). When he can find a clean pair of socks in the morning, not only have you averted a long 15 minute speech about how he "can't find anything in this house"…but you have also extinguished an opportunity for satan to come in and destroy your (and your husband's) day with stress and tension. Keep your own clothes neat and in good repair. Give away what you don't use. I did not say what you don't like. Although that is fine, if those things will still be useful to someone, but things you don't use and you haven't used since last year, give it away. Being a consistent pack rat is an outward sign that you believe no more is coming. It says to others, this is all I have and this is all I am going to get so I am going to hold on to it. Now, that does not sound like a member of royalty to me. You sound like a mere peasant. Get rid of excess and make room for the elevation and blessing of God. Get creative!! At my church, we have an annual Fashion Share program which is an awesome opportunity for us to give away women's clothes, jewelry, perfume, shoes etc.. to women in domestic violence shelters. Your children have uniforms from last year they can't fit. Have a uniform exchange with other parents at the school. Give to charitable organizations. Get that car that doesn't work out of the driveway and donate it to a charity program. Some programs will fix it up and sell it. The profits are used for community development and assistance. Trust me you will begin a continuous circle of sowing and reaping and God will always win. You cannot out give Him.

People at work should be able to look at the elegance and meticulousness of a presentation or how clean the coffee room is and know that "Camille" must have done this. Your area at work, whether it is an office, a cubicle or a janitors closet should be clean, well kept, and in order. Your attendance, attitude, demeanor, conversation and integrity at the office are paramount to being viewed as someone that should be respected. You can't gossip and curse with your co-workers and then invite them to your church's Easter program.

Organize your bills and other paperwork. I find that a lettered accordion file works best for me. I can file stuff by alphabet whether it is a bill, a note from school, or a magazine article. I always know where to find things and I constantly remind myself to be diligent enough to file things promptly. There are many books that talk more about organizing and getting rid of clutter. The goal is again to live and operate in the spirit of excellence. Your home, business, job, marriage, family and ministry should all be representative of the fact that you are a cut above the rest. Every letter you type, every program you organize, every outfit you wear regardless of what you paid for it, should reflect excellence.

Learning to recognize and destroy enemy camps

The last area we want to cover in the offensive plan for running your kingdom, is dealing with the enemy. We know that satan is ultimately the enemy. There are people, situations and circumstances that are direct attacks to what you are trying to do in your kingdom for God's Kingdom. Recognizing satanic attacks was not always easy for me. I did not know that God was involved, it appeared that only the enemy was in control. I was not ever into drugs, smoking or alcohol therefore satan could not use that to get me. But contrary to what I believed, satan did not wait until my arrival to try to destroy my kingdom. He started a spiritual chess game. However God already knew the outcome and God just played it out to humiliate the enemy, give me victory in my life to bring him glory. satan started back with my grandmother, who gave birth to my mom and left her with her mother (my mom's grandmother). My mother grew up not knowing her dad. She lived with her grandparents in the middle of the civil rights movement. She experienced segregation first hand. So not only did her parents not want her, but neither did society. The enemy was already working to pick away at her self esteem and self worth. Check.

On the other side, God was working in the Stephens household with a little boy that wanted to go to church with Deacon Parker. Although tentative and a church goer himself, His dad allowed him to go and the little Stephens boy became saved and attended church on a regular basis. Checkmate. This little boy, who later became my dad, grew up fast and he worked everywhere. He worked, while his other brothers and sisters attended school. He didn't receive a high school or college education. Check. Back on the other side, God arranged for my mom to attend one of the best high schools of that time for exceptionally bright children. Checkmate. This game continued until they were married and had children. My mom's experience and neglect from her father cause her to be a hard core woman. She is loving and giving and would sacrifice her last for you, but catch her in a bad moment and she would take you down. She was very independent and it was difficult for her to be trusting of men. She had very few models of what a good godly man was to be like. When she finally did catch up with her father, she was grown and married with children. What she found though did nothing to boost her ideology. Her father was an alcoholic living with a woman, in a pest-infected apartment in the worst part of town. My parents kept a roof over our heads, I always remember having enough to eat and I honestly had no idea I was poor, until I went to college. They did what they could with what they had. That was a characteristic that I am glad I picked up. They are survivors. Also, they kept God in front of us. Even when they were at each other's throats, we weren't sure if they loved each other, but we knew they loved God.

Eventually after experiencing and overcoming more tricks of the enemy, my mom struggled to get to know and love her dad and my dad was called into ministry. However, the stress of ministry and the pressures of intense study, and visitation and church services kept my dad gone a lot and the children left alone with my mom. My mom was the one working everyday, keeping the house, taking us to band practice, getting us to rehearsals, checking homework, usher board meeting, pressing hair, going to the market and cooking us dinner. My dad was busy studying, working, and going back to school. He eventually not only graduated high school but college as well. We were church babies and at church all the time for everything. My mom loved her dad right out of that apartment into an Alabama home. She also took care of her grandmother in our home. In the meantime our lives were pretty scheduled. This lifestyle, though with it good points as well, left me void of an example of the ideal of godly family structuring. My mom was exhausted and irritated. My dad was not involved much in our lives and the importance of male confirmation for a daughter is overwhelming. He didn't know. I didn't know. He probably didn't have an example of that either. Satan had him so busy with surviving; all he had time to learn was how to keep his head above water. My mom didn't know, she had a void in that area as well. I sought that confirmation or covering in everyone and everything. Whether it was a boyfriend, or a project at school or work. I stayed busy all the time. In my senior year, I worked, went to school, was on the yearbook staff, editor of the newspaper staff, the marching band, the church choir and the usher board. I was also cold, hard, mean, non trusting and standoffish. I could play the role, but was very "anti-folk". I was driven, but didn't really like people very much. I was in essence, both my parents when they were younger, rolled into one person. When I got married at 19, I had a baby and a man I thought would cover me, protect me, affirm me, teach me and be a spiritual head for me. Turn to your neighbor and say "bonehead move". Satan had set up an enemy camp and I fell into the trap hook line and sinker. At 19, I was clueless as to what marriage was all about. I had no business marrying him or anyone else. I was immature and not ready at all for the issues and temptations we would face. There were things as a single that I should have done first. I did not know the seriousness of the commitment. More importantly, I did not know the ramifications of marrying an unbeliever. I didn't understand that without a sanctified husband, it would be easy for me to slip, get off track and fall into the traps time after time. I didn't understand that any children we had would be subject to any curse that ran in his family. I didn't realize that expecting something from him that he could not deliver was wrong. I had a new baby, a new husband, a new marriage but an old problem. God was not at the center of that union. It was a trick of the enemy to give me a false sense of security and well being. He thought to get me to a place of complacency where I would continue to settle for less what he had for me.

After three more children and seven shaky years, the marriage was over. I wish my children's father nothing but the best. Any damage I may have caused in life, I have asked God to restore. However, he was not my destiny. Choosing to get married at that time was a back alley path and I was way off track. I was not on God's road for me and I knew better. He has since that time remarried and he took care of our oldest son during his senior year. I remind my children to pray continuously for his total reconciliation back to God, so he can be the man God has called him to be. Now, needless to say I got four awesome, fun, incredibly cute children out of the deal. For a long time, they were the only reason I stayed alive. God used them to keep me and I am forever grateful for them. Satan kept me distracted in "surviving". 4 kids, a single mom and poverty, don't mix. But satan was already at work into the next generation. He thought, get the man out of Jerica's (my daughter) life and she will fall into the same trap that her mom did. I started seeing things in those kids that I had never seen or thought about doing in my life. Some stuff I recognized. The issues that my siblings and I dealt with, I could handle.

However, there were some demons operating perhaps from their dad's family that I had not encountered before. But you see, someone in their dads' family would recognize it. **Again, be mindful of who you have attached yourself to**. I heard this revelation just in time and started the fight for my family. satan thought he had my kids. Turn to your neighbor again and say, not gonna happen! He figured my boys would grow up trifling, irresponsible, and disrespectful to women...NOT SO !! You see I found the camp and rooted it out. I dug and dug into my own mess far enough to see where it came from so it can be rooted out. What I couldn't find in me I turned the rest over to the Lord. It was not a pretty process. I didn't like the digging, admitting or dealing with my past issues. You have to want to be delivered from the trap bad enough to be willing to face the cause, repent, and accept responsibility. I hold my children to a higher standard because of what I have fought for on their behalf. They know what happens if you are having sex before marriage. They know the stupidity, selfishness and irresponsibility of getting married to someone, just because you had a baby and not because that is who God intends for you to have. The world would tell you to marry him or her is the "responsible" thing to do. I tell my children it's a trap -don't listen. They know what can happen if you do marry the wrong person and end up getting a divorce. They know firsthand the cycle and pain of being in lack, insecure or unstable. Tell your children about the enemy camps. Tell them the curses that ran rampant in your family and how you have wedged a shield of protection in prayer covering them and redeeming from that generational foolishness. Proclaim to them and around your house that no seed will come forth from your children outside of the covenant of a God ordained marriage. No one else in my lineage will be affected by the wiles of the devil that took place in my family before I got here. Tell them to tell their children that the curse stopped with Nana Camille. Will my children error? Yep. Will it be in this area, the chances are slimmer, not because they are perfect nor am I, but because I am in their face and God's face all the time about it. If they should fall, it will not be because of lack of information, lack of example or not knowing that they have the power to fight against the temptation. I remind them that "I love you" is not always shown in an "act of doing" whether it is sex, or giving a gift or doing someone a favor. It is also shown in what you **won't** do. Because you love yourself, your bishop or pastor, your parents, the person you are "dating" and GOD, you will sacrifice what your flesh wants to do and exchange that with what is best for them and what is godly.

    My daughter will tell you in a minute, she can't be sexually impure because she is not "cursed". She was younger and may not have understood what that meant, but she knew it was bad. She knows not to just listen to anything a guy tells her, but watch what he does. I tell her "Don't **play** hard to get, **BE** hard to get". If he will try to take you beyond your boundaries, he is expressing utter disrespect for you. He does not love you, he can't. If you seduce him, **you** are acting self-centered, selfish and inconsiderate of what

God wants to do in his life and yours. Those are not characteristics of a godly wife, and if he is godly he should want no part of you (at least until you mature) and should continue his search for a virtuous woman somewhere else because you aren't ready. I told my son, getting a girl pregnant when you know what is right not only jeopardizes your destiny and who God intends for you to have, but it demonstrates "the spirit of stupid" in your life and it is severely selfish and disrespectful to the young lady, her parents, your sisters, me, your Bishop, ….He was like ma, I know "spirit of stupid" I got it. He is probably tired of hearing it. So! Anytime it is placed in my spirit to remind them or tell them a situation I was in, they will hear it again. These are hard sayings, but oh well. This is my kingdom and that's my job. As for me and my house we will serve the Lord. Diana Ross had a song "It's my house, and I live here!" Laugh if you want, but you can sing this to enemy and tell him that both of us can't stay. It's MY house and I live here and in my house we have chosen this day whom we will serve.

But guys this is only **one** area. As much work as it took to plant these seeds in this area, there are others that I have missed. There are other places where they have fallen short. I pray all the time for the Spirit to make up the difference. There is more work to be done. Unveil the camp, whatever it is. It could be alcoholism, gambling, workaholic tendencies, irresponsible with money, cantankerous with men, selfishness, being phony or pretentious. Knowledge is power.

Remember Slim? When she figured out that the motive of her enemy was to kill her, she had to step up her game. Princess, satan is not out to try to make your life uncomfortable. He is trying to kill you and your seed. He wants to put enough stuff in the mix so you'll be promiscuous and needy enough to sleep with any guy and eventually get AIDS and die early. He wants to pile on so many issues and scare tactics and couple that with your past, that you will eat wrong, not take care of your body and kill yourself. He wants a single mom to have to work two jobs to make ends meet, so she can't instill godly principles in her children or go to get the Word herself and die unsaved. He is manipulating the lives of others just to get to you. He is not content with just you. He wants to ruin your witness in front of your children, neighbors and family to destroy

God's credibility. Tear down the tents in the enemy camp. Face your issues and those passed down to you. Fight for your kingdom!

Reflection and Application

1. Study the life of a royal (Biblical or Secular). Learn what they stood for (positively or negatively). Study sacrifices made or battles won to allow them to rule their kingdom effectively. Example: Grace Kelly sacrificed a Hollywood movie career and her citizenship and home in the United States to marry Prince Ranier of Monoco. Princess Grace Kelly was the most beloved princess and starlet of her time. Her daughters are now princesses in the land and they continue her legacy.

2. Look for the "Chess game" in your life. What strategies did the enemy intend for evil, but worked out for good? Remember areas where the devil set up and God delivered you, in spite of you. Always remember that God has the last move.

3. What generational tendencies do you see in your family (parents, grandparents, aunts, uncles, cousins etc..) that seem to be a common thread (positive or negative) throughout the family. For example, it could be poverty, wealth, the ability to sing or act, strong willed women, incarcerated men, entrepreneurs, spousal abuse, children out of wedlock, divorce, diabetes, heart conditions, high blood pressures). Which generational tendencies are operating in your life (positive or negative)?

4. Begin to separate the blessings from the curses and rebuke the enemy off of those areas in your life and the lives of your children. For example here's a prayer I pray over my children now:

Lord, I come against the spirit of promiscuity in my family. My children are redeemed from the curse of sexual impurity. I pray no seed will be brought forth that is not covered under the divine order you have set. I pray in advance over their spouses to-be. My children and their spouses will be

God-fearing, spirit filled, wise, and loving men and women of God. Their spouses will love my children with an unselfishness and unsurpassing love. Cover them and protect them from the assignments of the enemy. I pray for their parents that they are godly, spirit filled and instilling in them qualities they will need to be helpmeets and rulers of destiny. My children and their spouses-to-be will be godly examples of marriage and family. My grandchildren and their children will remember this blessing and claim it in their own lives and the lives of their children after them. This curse is now and forever broken in Jesus name and I bless my family with healthy relationships, anointed marriages and blessed children.

Pray a prayer of blessing over you and your family. Pronounce that curse dead in Jesus name.

CHAPTER SIX

Get Nanny's Purse !

After school was prime time for many events. The rush to get to Ms. Eileen's penny store, to the race to the school bus to get the "good" seats. It was also a time where most school fights took place.

During the course of the day some minor altercation or bullying attempt will take place that will end with the most feared promise in elementary school. With fist drawn up ... your opponent looks you in the eye and mouths three syllables that have the power to coward even the strongest third grader "THREE- O- CLOCK". Translated: I plan to beat you into the ground as soon as the bell rings.

I have had two such threats. The funny thing is nothing ended in a fight. The first one my friend Vicki stood up for me and told Satira (funny, I still remember that name) that she'd have to fight both of us and in the second case nobody showed up for the fight. However, in both of these cases I spent the day being very afraid. I was afraid to walk the hall by myself. In the lunchroom, I looked for a friendly face and sat with them. I was too scared to talk much. I spent time and time again looking at the clock and dreading my afternoon classes. By my last scheduled class, I was a nervous wreck. My heart was beating out of my chest. My palms were sweaty. I had this pit feeling in my stomach that just ached. I felt like I was constantly on the verge of tears. I was antsy and fidgety.

A Princess-Cut Diamond

Honestly, just plain scared. I wasn't afraid to fight. I'm an Eastside Detroit girl. I didn't mind fighting, still don't. It's the injury part that I am not fond of. I couldn't stand the thought of my face being scratched or my arm being broken. Not that I would lose, but in any fight you are subject to take a hit. My fear was based on what I had to go through to win rather than the victory itself.

In actuality fear of the "assumed" is a major tool of the enemy. He practically paralyzes us until we finally see that whatever we were dreading either wasn't as bad, or didn't happen as we thought it would. During the time of fear which can be one day or ten years, we are totally non productive in that area. We are afraid to move forward and afraid to turn back. We know we should have done something about our thought life but fear had us too scared to move. For example, we think our car is going to be repossessed so we don't call to make arrangements because we are afraid before it even happens. We think our lights aren't gonna be on when we get home. We assume we are going to be single forever. We think prosperity is never coming and we dread the reality of being poor. We don't go back to school because we think we can't graduate. If the energy that is spent on dread/fear could actually be channeled into changing our assumed destiny the enemy would lose a major stronghold in our lives. Now (that I know, that is) if someone was to bully me and say "three o clock"....I'd look back and say "Bring it !"

Is that because I am not going to get beat up? No, because I might...but the truth is I am no longer afraid that I may lose. I am not afraid of getting scratched. If I have to fight poverty, divorce, low self esteem, addictions.. then ok..let's rumble. My kingdom is worth the fight. I am no longer stuck in the fear of "this is gonna happen and there is nothing I can do." Since the battle belongs to the Lord, my thought is I'm gonna give him what's rightfully his. He can have it. Every battle, every fight, every scrimmage-it's his to control. My job is to show up, stand still and see the salvation of the Lord. But um, you DO have to show up.

As a Princess, you will have to go to war sometimes. There may be times when your children will walk in disobedience. Your boyfriend may have a stanky attitude. Your husband may not be acting godly. Your boss may treat you unfairly and your co-workers may set you up for a fall. You will have to fight for your integrity. You will need to fight to remain godly when someone is on your last nerve. You will have to fight for your reputation, whether they told the truth or a lie. You will fight to walk holy. There will be times that the fight you will have will be with yourself. You may have done something you know disappointed God. You may not be tithing like you should. You could have snapped at your children because you're tired or not have ministered to your husband, or friends like you should have. Finances, disappointments, death, anger, lack of self control, pride and foolishness will seek to destroy your kingdom. You will have to fight to not get discouraged or disillusioned. You'll have to fight when you are tired of fighting.

Regardless of the virtual opponent, the actual enemy is satan. You have to fight him with the weapons that will defeat him. The Bible says that the weapons of our warfare are not carnal. You can't do what the world does and expect to defeat the enemy and preserve your kingdom. Which means, regardless of what he did you cannot curse him out. You can't beat your child over spilled kool-aid. You have to discern the difference between a mistake, rebellion and a total disregard to godliness. You can't approach your job, your marriage, your parents, your home, or your neighborhood using the world's strategy. The world fights differently, and for different reasons. You have to believe that the battle is the Lord's. You have to stand on the fact that God expects you to show up and stand up against the enemy, but it is God and His Spirit through you and others that will defeat him. You have to learn HOW to fight and with what weapons.

My Grandmother, affectionately called "Nanny" carries a gun. There is nothing we can do about it. There is nothing to say about it. She has it and if you mess with one of her children or grandchildren, she had no problem using it. She usually keeps it in her purse and it could be the cutest little clutch church bag, but you better believe that thing is packing some power. When something "goes down" in our family and Nanny is present, we know the importance of getting Nanny's purse 1st. It may look little and unassuming, but in that little tote carries the power to take you out.

We are going to go over a few weapons, some of which you

may not have ever thought of as being a weapon. You may think of them as simple and unassuming, but just like Nanny's purse, if you pull them out they will pack a punch beyond measure. Examples will show you how incredibly mighty they are. Prayer, encouragement, standing and rest are the "guns" we going to use to guard our kingdom.

Prayer

Most women have an extraordinary inherited gift of communication. When we want something, we know how to talk our way into it. Not manipulation, but we have the ability to remember information long enough to use it when it is necessary. You know that in the midst of a heated discussion with a significant other, we can bring up things they did when they were 8 years old, what they had on, and their facial expression when they did it, if it would plead our case. Believe it or not, God gave us that skill for a reason. It was not an arrow intended for our husbands or to discourage our friends or children, but a tool to use in prayer to God.

That is why it is imperative that we find out what God has said, remember it and store it in that awesome memory bank of ours and pray back His Word to Him in every situation. Think back to the Word and remember who went through what and pray that back to God. I am one of the first to say, Ok God YOU said that my sons and daughters will prophesy. YOU are the one that said that if I fear you that my seed shall be mighty upon the earth. Lord, I am not seeing mighty here. I am not seeing vessels that will prophesy. I am not moved by what I see. I walk in faith. In faith, I see an enemy stronghold and I come against it now in Jesus name. This situation must line up with the WORD. You have deemed it so and so it is. Open my eyes God, give me the wisdom you promised if I ask for it.

Trust me I will call God on his promises. Usually what that does is cause me to confess out of my mouth what it truth instead of what I see. It makes me to remember what God has said and gives me hope. Now if you pray God's word, you must believe that whatever you have prayed (believing that you have received it) you shall have it. In order to come to God, the Bible says that you must first believe that God is, or that God exists AND believe that He is a rewarder of them that diligently seek Him. We should ask knowing that God has to do what He said He would do or God would be a liar and He cannot lie. We pray sometimes like we are shooting dice as in…"this may work…it may not"…but remember contrary to popular opinion…God cannot do **whatever** He wants to do. He bound **HIMSELF** to His Word and He has to do what He said He would do. His timing and His method are His to control. But be mindful, his promises are a contracted deal. So regardless of the situation it is imperative to the survival of your kingdom to know what God said and pray back to Him what He said. His Word cannot return void. He has to do what He told you He would do. Be mindful that His promises are true but His judgments are true as well. If God has conditioned a promise, don't think you can skirt around it. For example, you can't pray Lord you promised that I would eat the good of the land. The scripture you are referencing says that IF you are WILLING and OBEDIENT THEN you will eat the good of the land. Make sure you have clarity about your responsibility before you ask God to keep His end of the bargain. Now if you are in the hole and you need help and you know you were in the wrong, repent. If it was someone else that was wrong, intercede on his or her behalf if necessary. There is grace to cover you in time of need.

Encouragement

My circle of friends have a saying "Encourage yourself, David did". We usually say it when somebody is acting a tad pitiful and wants everybody to come to the pity party. We don't say it to be mean, however sometimes people you have to "suck it up". Stop the drama, put your lip in, wipe your face and handle your business! We often use friends and loved ones around us all the time to lift us up, bail us out and pump us up, but you have to know and understand that as a royal, there will be many times that you will be alone. You will look around and see that people are busy and have their own lives. Sometimes you can't be propped up by what others think or feel. You have to just gut it out and quit being a whiny girl. There is no whining in a crown. Let's look at David and see why he, The King, had to find it within himself to be encouraged.

In 1 Samuel 30 we learn that David had just left the Philistines.

He and his army were on the way back home to Ziklag. When they returned, they found that the Amalekites had raided their camp. They not only took their belongings, but the enemy took their wives and children as captives and burned everything down. A key that you may miss is in verse 2. It reads that "And (the Amalekites) had taken the women and all who were there both great and small captive...THEY KILLED NO ONE, but carried them off and went on their way" AMP. Let me just take a sidebar to tell you that your child may be out in the street, but if they are still alive you can still fight for them. You may have lost that job, but if you can still work, you can still fight to be employed. Your relative may still be on drugs, but if they haven't overdosed you can intercede for them. You may have messed up a relationship, but if you are still alive, you can resolve the matter even if it is with yourself. If there is still life in a situation, victory is still possible. Be also aware that God can take what is dead and revive it. If there was dream you had and you have shelved it, God can resurrect it. A person you thought you would never see saved, will start asking you about the Word of God. Just because YOU deem it dead does not mean that it is. God can move in any situation.

David and his men had a good old-fashioned snot-cry. David was also getting fearful, not only because of what had happened but because now the men were talking about stoning him. I supposed if you are like me, you can remember many times that you have messed up so bad that it affected everyone around you. You were sure that if your children really knew what you did they'd be ready to turn you in for a new improved mom. You have been in a position that your antics, mishaps, mistakes or issues through no fault of your own have caused others hardship, pain or loss. It's a very hard place to be. People that should love you will hate you out of their own hurt. They are disappointed, point at you and blame you for their current lot in life. On top of that, you are dealing with your own hurt and grieving your own loss of possessions, people, status, position or stability. Remember David's stuff was gone as well as his wives along with everyone else's stuff. So he was coming to grips with happened, plus dealing with the guilt trip that the men were seeking to put on him. At this point, David could have done many things. He could have run. In the middle of the night David could have left the group and spent his days as a wanted man for the rest of his life. He could have just thrown himself at the men and gave his life up to be stoned. He could have flown off the handle at them and rebuked them for wanted to kill their "leader". He could have just laid there and kept crying. But the Bible says that David **encouraged** and strengthened himself in the Lord. Nobody around him was singing that "David has killed tens of thousand" song then. Samuel wasn't there. His best friend Jonathan wasn't there. People who wanted to kill him surrounded him. Remember, David himself has lost his wife, children and possessions too. No one was bowing talking about "your majesty" either. David had to remember the goodness of the Lord and turn to the Lord for himself when things got bad. **After** he encouraged himself, he got strength. He had strength enough to ask the Lord two very important questions. 1) Lord, shall I pursue this troop? David was encouraged and ready to go after the enemy. He needed direction and permission from God. He couldn't afford to make any more mistakes. **LEARN THIS-** After a major screw up, Princess **DON'T MOVE** without direction from God or godly counsel. 2) Lord, shall I overtake them? David was flat out honest with God. He needed to know up front if he was going to win. I supposed if God said no, he would have told the men that God said that this was a battle they could not win. God, of course told him to pursue and he would definitely overtake them. Not only did David pursue the enemy, he got help from someone formally in the enemy camp. He got back all of the wives and children. He got back all of his stuff and the things that belonged to his men.

Prayer is a powerful weapon, but what you pray is like bullets. When you encounter something, we have a tendency to pray for strength. Strength is not always what you need. Sometimes you may just need encouragement or exhortation. Sometimes you just need guts. You need the desire to see yourself in a better situation. You need the inner will to be out of where you are and into where God will have you to be. Sometimes you just need to pray that God will stop the tears and drama long enough for you to see your next step clear. Princess, it is time to wipe your nose and encourage your doggone self. If your girlfriend ain't home and your prayer partner didn't return your call, what are you gonna do? Cry out to the Lord...all pitiful like? Aw Lawd....just give me strength to make it until I can reach Sheila on the phone? I don't think so. How about, "I am sick of this!!" "Lord, give me the will to line up with your will for my life. Give me the desire to bootstrap it up!! You said to pursue. You said I would win. I will go forth in Jesus name." Tell yourself how awesome you are. That's right talk to yourself! Remind yourself of other situations you have made it through. Speak out the blessing you know is ahead for you. Get up girl... and encourage yourself...David did.

Stand

We have heard the popular scriptures on standing. "Having done all to stand, stand therefore…" Or, "stand still and see the salvation of the Lord." We still sometimes lack the understanding of how to stand and how to use it as a weapon against the enemy. The best way I can describe it would be a story I heard about two famous boxers. The Thrilla in Manilla is said to be one of the most brutal matches in history. Both fighters fought hard and long. They were both exhausted and worn out. By round ten both fighters showed clear signs of fatigue, fighting at low pace. In Joe's corner, the trainers and coaches sat him down and started wiping him off, tending to his wounds and giving him water. They were telling him what he could do to make it through the next round, but Joe was weary and struggling to pay attention. In Muhammad Ali's corner, when he went to sit down the trainer moved the stool and said, "**Stand up champ!**".

He was so exhausted that he could barely stand, so Ali stood up as straight as he could and then he just leaned on the ropes. It is said that Joe looked over and saw Ali standing and figured that if he could still stand after over two hours of fighting, he had more left in him than he did. Ali's ability to stand intimidated Joe.

Ali's trainer Angelo Dundee said after the fight: "Both guys ran out of gas, only my guy had an extra tank". Where Ali received the energy to come back in the heat and humidity of the Coliseum and hit Frazier more intensely than anyone had hit him before, has been subject to theory ever since. "Ali's magic" appeared for what is said was the last time in his career. From round twelve on, Frazier doesn't land a hit. In round thirteen his mouthpiece is knocked out of his mouth and out of the ring. So did his chance to win the fight. By round fourteen, Joe's left eye is completely shut so that he is not able to see Ali throwing a right hand any more.

In the break before the last round, Frazier's trainer Eddie Futch stops the fight. Too dominating, too far ahead had Ali been on the scorecards. Joe Frazier was too handicapped in terms of his vision to have any chance of winning. Moments after the fight was over, **Ali fainted in his corner**. No one knows whether he could have resumed the fight. Ali was later quoted that **he had been ready to quit if Joe had not.** Could you imagine how Joe Frazier felt hearing that? He probably said, if I could have just held out a little longer, I would have been the champion!

I tell my children "Many of life's failures are people who did not realize how close they were to success when they gave up." You could be right at the point of your breakthrough and you go sit in your corner and pout. Stand up Champ!! Ali held it together until he won the fight and so can you. The Bible says to "Let us not be weary in well doing, for in due season we shall reap if we faint not. Ali knew when to relax. It was AFTER he won the fight. But when he was still in the battle he stood strong and did not faint.

Standing is a powerful weapon! Your persistence will drive the enemy mad. If you will still go to morning worship after dealing with an unbelieving spouse, you are standing. If you will pray over your child, even when they are disobedient and defiant you are standing. If you can still sow financial seeds even when your resources are few, you are standing. When you are faithful at work and to your boss, even when the management is iniquitous and doesn't keep its promises, you are standing. If you can look at a doctor that has just given you a bad report, and say "Thank you, I shall believe the report of the Lord" you are standing.

One further instruction in standing that is used in scripture is stand "still". Sometimes your biggest arsenal is the power to do nothing, even when your flesh screams 'what are you gonna do?'. Sometimes God will call upon you to stand STILL and that requires just as much power as it does to purpose to do something.

The children of Israel were told to stand still at the red sea. They had a sea in front of them and Pharaoh behind them. But most importantly they had a God above them. When God got them to a place where they couldn't move, He was able to move supernaturally on their behalf.

Rest

"Git somewhere and sat down !" Grammatically that sentence may not have been correct, however I am willing to bet that most of you have heard that statement ring out of the mouth of a mother, grandmother, a church mother, or Mrs. Mayberry next door. Have you ever dealt with a child who has not had their nap for the day or they are extremely bored? They are almost impossible to tolerate. The whining, the complaining, the questions, the nit-picky "he touched my finger" temper tantrum attitude is enough to send anyone reeling.

Are we there yet?

Mom, I have to go to the bathroom.

Dad, I'm hungry.

I'm bored.

She's hitting me !!!

Are we there yet?

Any parent would be able to recognize these statements as the infamous "road trip whines". Children, with their boundless source of energy want to know two things on a trip. First, are we there yet and if not what can I do in the meantime to keep busy such as go to the bathroom, eat, play, pick at my sister etc… As a driver, your neck gets stiff, your eyes glaze over into a daydream, your foot cramps, and your back begins to hurt.

When the restlessness or "tiredness" gets too bad, you have to decide whether to pull over at the next rest area or keep going. I try to push as long as I can. My goal is to make it to the destination. But, if we have a ways to go and I feel my condition is a hazard, I stop and allow the children and myself to re-group. I get a coffee, check my map, go to the bathroom, stretch, eat something and then get back on the highway.

As a Princess in training, I come to realize that if some of us would pull over and rest a minute, we can re-group and be ready to proceed on our journey rested and alert. When you are beginning to notice small nitpicky attacks from the enemy or if things that normally don't bother you start to annoy you or cause you to get off balance, it may be time to pull over at a rest area. Your focus is getting blurred. Those things also serve as definite clues that a "timeout" won't hurt.

What does resting in the Lord mean? How much time it takes isn't relevant. Everybody is different. It's a matter of reminding yourself, who is really in control. It's taking time to reflect on your destination and purpose in ministry. It's a release of all anxieties of not being good enough, not having enough, or not knowing enough. A simple renewing of your belief that God is God.

Is this journey getting a little stressful for you? Are things coming at you from every side? Make a decision today to stand still and see the salvation of the Lord. Slow down and come to a stop. Don't tackle anything today that isn't an ABSOLUTE must. Cast your cares on Jesus because he cares for you. Regroup; review your map (purpose). Make sure you are on the right track to get there. Eat the word, study and give your journey to God in prayer.

Start being mindful of what you say "yes" to. Do you really need to be president of the PTA again this year? Can you not be in this year's Christmas program and still go to heaven? Do you have to have the kids in choir, usher board, Jr. Missionaries, gymnastics, skating, tutoring and tennis?

We underestimate how being tired can effect your thinking and your faith. A perfect example would be Samson who after a great victory was so exhausted that simple thirst led him into a state of depression. Judges 15:18 says "Because he (Samson) was very thirsty, he cried out to the Lord, "You have given your servant this great victory. Must I now die of thirst and fall into the hands of the uncircumcised?" NIV. Samson had gotten physically and emotionally tired. It can become easy for you to fall into a pity party after overcoming a major feat.

Sometimes our part in the battle wears us out to the point that we can't even enjoy the victory. We are already on to the next thing. I had a bad habit of doing that. As soon as I worked out how the light bill would be paid, instead being thankful for how God worked it out, I shoved it in the back of my mind and started on the next fight. Sometimes, though not all the time, I needed to just stop and look at how far God brought me and thank him for it, instead of checking it off my list and focusing my prayer time on the next problem.

In 1 Kings 19, Elijah had gotten tired and depressed after the defeat of the prophets of Baal. Jezabel was after him and he being tired and afraid ran from her. He came to a tree and sat there and prayed that he would die. He fell asleep and in Verse 5 it says an angel awakened him and told him to eat. This brings out two important points 1. God does not mind if you rest, the angel did not rebuke him for sleeping. 2. God **does** care if you do not take care of yourself physically and spiritually. He will provide even in the low times. You must eat in the physical sense. We know we have to eat right and take care of our bodies. In the spiritual sense, resting doesn't mean you can do without eating the Word of God. Just because you aren't singing in the choir this month, does not mean you are excused from Bible study.

In verse 6 there is an interesting point that can be overlooked as well. It tells us that Elijah awoke, ate and went back to sleep. Just because you are full of the Word does not mean that you are mentally and emotionally ready to go back into ministry. Let God release you back into the "workforce". Sometimes before running off "gung ho" into a project, it is best to just wait. After a resting period your spirit should be "quieter" and you should be better able to hear the voice of God and his direction. You may need a little more rest from the daily shuffle and the tedious scheduling that we can put **ourselves** through. But listen closely, because when it is time to roll out…its time to roll out. In verse 8, it says, "he arose, ate and went. Elijah was full rested and ready to go. God was able to then lead him to a place where he could be instructed and restored.

As comfortable as a rest stop is, Princess don't stay there parked forever. Relaxing isn't permanent, although a "state of rest" is. Keep your mind stayed on Jesus and his promise is to keep you in perfect peace. You take the time to get what you need and prepare to move on. Then, rested, refreshed and reenergized…get back on the road and ride on to what God has in store for you.

Reflection and Application

1. What do you need in order to feel encouraged? Is your list a list of people? Does include habits like shopping or eating? What if those things or people aren't around?

2. What can you do if it was just you alone and you needed to be encouraged? Can you sing a song, read the Word or talk yourself out of a depression?

3. Is there anything or anyone in your life that has been taken into the enemy camp that you need to pursue? Is there a dream or a situation you think is dead but would like God to resurrect?

4. How do you react when you are at fault or you are the focus of the blame?

5. How do you react when you are tired, or need to rest? How can you let go of control in some areas of your life, in order to rest and refocus on your kingdom?

Learn Jeremiah 33:3

Call unto me and I will answer thee and show thee great and mighty things, which thou knowest not.

CHAPTER SEVEN

The Big Fat Princess

Diaper Bag and purse on one shoulder, crying, heavy infant wrapped in the other arm. Your hands are full with keys, coupons, pacifier, grocery list, sales paper and some tissue. You get to the door of the supermarket and as you step on the mat the door automatically opens. You are able to easily walk on through to a cart and set up to begin your shopping experience without dropping anything.

Now imagine you're carrying a large box out of a building and as you approach the door you realize that the door is a revolving type door and you and the box will not fit. You have three choices:

Leave the box and go through the door.

Make the load smaller, more manageable and attempt to squeeze through.

Find a different, bigger, easier door, usually further away from your intended destination.

This princess path is quite a journey. I must tell you now beloved to save you the time and trouble…EVERYTHING CAN'T GO!! There are some things and people that will be left behind. There have been times in your past that God has allowed you to take your little red wagon of issues with you. That time is drawing to a close. To whom much is given, much is required. The more knowledge you acquire the more you are called to act upon what you know. You must drop some of the weight you have been carrying.

During your reign as a Princess, you will approach doors of decision, doors of opportunity and doors of emotion all the time. Some doors open "automatically" because of God's timing, purposes or promises. We are able to walk through dragging our issues and hang-ups with us. As a new believer, God allows leniency in areas. You aren't responsible for all the things you have not understood yet. He will continue to hold you up and bless you until you get through the "new stage". If you step out in certain areas, God will meet you there and open the door for you. You will find that even though you are still smoking cigarettes and you slip back into partying every once in awhile, God will not discount you as being his. You are still a baby. He keeps you in the family and your issues come with you. He is not shocked or surprised at what he is getting. He knew you and knew what you were struggling with when he saved you.

You may remember Rahab, who is still known and listed in the Bible as "Rahab, the Harlot". God used her and saved her and her family in spite of her current "occupation". She is the great grandmother of Jesus Christ and *that lady was a tramp*. God did not require that she go get cleaned up before he used her for his purpose. He used her in spite of her, dragging issues through the door. Because of Rahab's obedience, God blessed her and through her seed, salvation came into the world through Jesus Christ. So trust me when I tell you, your issues don't intimidate God. IF YOU FEAR HIM, as Rahab did, he will work around your shortcomings and get you to the place of destiny.

Moses is another example. He was getting instruction from God and coming up with excuses as to why he wasn't the best person for the job. He reasoning was, that God wanted to use him as a prolific speaker but he had a speech impediment. I am sure God said to himself "no kidding...I would not have known that had you not told me". But God in his mercy, told Moses and his speech impediment to go and take Aaron with him.

Gideon, however takes the cake in this area. In the book of Judges, not only did Gideon give God a sign and wonder test before he would obey God. But when God performed it, Gideon asked him to do it again; to be sure it wasn't a coincidence. Even before that when God first came to him and told him to deliver Israel from the hand of the Midianites, Gideon got his issues list rolling. He said, why are we in this situation in the first place? He was upset about being under the Midianites to begin with. However, the 1st verse in chapter 6 was very clear as to why " And Israel again did evil in the sight of the Lord'. Then he said he couldn't do it because his tribe (Manasseh) was the smallest one. God finally said **go in the might (or the strength) that you have.** That's a lesson for someone reading this now. You are waiting for all of the ducks to line up in a row, God has told you to go. You are trying to make sure you have everything together, God has told you to do this. You want all of your issues to be handled before you can be used of God when God has said that you can do all things through Christ. You want to wait until you have your pornography issue under control. You would rather be sure that you wouldn't get angry or jealous anymore first. You don't feel you know enough or that you are smart enough, pretty enough, know all the right people, or have enough support. God says **go in the might that you have.** Princess, work with what you have. If God has sent you into a project, he is obligated to equip you to handle it. He will put you where you need to be even if you are dragging your issues with you. That's a word for me as well. There are situations that I am facing, that I don't always feel I have the grace to conquer. I would much rather wait until I am confident that I can handle what will come. But that does not require faith, and *without faith* it is **impossible to please God.** That means THERE IS NO CHANCE whatsoever to please, gratify or delight God without having faith in His ability. I have to go in the strength I have and trust God to make up the difference.

    Even with me, and this book. I asked God as Moses did (in the 10 commandments movie anyway), "who am I that they will listen"? I know what Moses felt when he asked, "They will ask me your name and what should I tell them"? In other words, "I ain't all that sure about everything about you, and when other people ask me who can I tell them you are that they will understand?" He said write and I have to assume God knew whom He was talking to and what I have or don't have. When I got to the door, he opened it up....issues and all.

In other areas where I should have more faith through experience with God, it is not as easy. As your relationship develops with God, His expectations will increase. When faced with a closed or narrow door, the easiest thing to do it would seem, is drop our box of what "we think" and simply think about what God has done and can do, do it and walk on through. But instead, we try to think of a way of taking our box of doubt, fear, unbelief, carnal thinking and ungodly character with us. That no longer works in this phase. Princess, you will stay right in that circle until you pass this test. The same issues you brought up to God before will not work here.

Imagine if Moses was standing at the Red Sea and God tells him to stretch out his staff and Moses replies "But God, I still have this speech problem and...." God would have had every right to take that staff and knock Moses in the head with it. Think about it, after 1, 2,3, 4, 5, 6, 7, 8, 9, **10** supernatural plagues against Egypt, including killing all of their firstborn and sparing all of Israel's firstborn, to send a giant pillar of fire to guide them and block the Egyptians, to walk 1 million people PLUS, out of slavery all the way to this point...and this same God tells you to lift up a stick and you tell him you can't talk !! You sound crazy!! You say, well God didn't ask him to talk so that does sound foolish. EXACTLY.

What God has for you do to, has nothing to do with what you can't do, except to know that YOU KNOW that you could not have done it without him. In this stage of your relationship, God has proven himself to you, over and over again. Your doubt and unbelief ain't cute. As a Princess, you have to know enough about God and be in fellowship with him so intimately that you can leave your bags and boxes of hesitation on the other side and walk in trust on the path he has designed for you.

Somewhere in the middle of our thinking is another strategy. We try to drop a box here and there...make our load *appear* smaller by maybe forgiving but not forgetting. Or maybe we believe God for his choice for a mate, but will settle for the one that's unsaved or backslidden because he's here and available. We will earnestly fast and pray for an answer and when one does not come in our timing, we will have a plan B waiting in the wings.

One biblical account tells us that David, when he was preparing for a battle, he was obedient to go and fight. But first he started counting people in his army. As if the number of people had something to do with the victory. He got penalized for that, and so will you. You cannot be half in and half out. Trusting God over here and doing things your own way in this area won't work. I am talking to myself as well. I have big faith that God can fix "this" issue but when it comes to something else, I have the nerve to doubt his power.

Or lastly, we try to go out another way. Usually this is a back way. In our "door scenario" the other way is normally not meant for regular traffic. It could be a freight elevator or the maintenance door. It is most likely farther away from where you were intending on going. In your decision-making processes, this is the way the enemy prefers for you to take. His way is the back-alley way, as in, just lie on your taxes it won't matter. Or, just call him-your husband will never find out. His back door allows you to hold on to your anger, resentment, and bitterness as if it wouldn't have an effect on your relationships. You're feeling down and depressed and instead of seeking God, you spend money you don't have at the mall or go out for a night of partying and drinking with the girls and then just pray with all earnest on Sunday Morning. Just look at Sampson. I'm sure his friends told him…Delilah is nice. She can't hurt a flea. Even though his parents told him what type of woman he should be with, his back alleyway through Delilah cost him his anointing, his witness and his strength.

The Word of God says that the His way is narrow. Which is to simply imply, that everything can't travel with you. Some of us are simply just too "fat" with issues that we can't fit on HIS path comfortably. Excessive loads, burdens, cares, and old, heavy baggage weren't designed for the Princess journey. I know you want to take your jealousy, gluttony, selfishness and envy with you, but some things you have to leave at the door or you won't be able to move. Jesus says, "I am the door". Therefore today decide to lay aside every weight that will so easily set you back at the foot of Jesus and walk on through the door of your destiny.

Reflection and Application

1. What past "occupations" or labels are attached to you that are blocking your ability to believe that God can use you?

2. In what areas of your life have you walked in compromise? What can you do TODAY to begin to straighten up these bends in the road?

3. What excuses have you given to God as to why you couldn't walk in obedience? Can you look past your insecurities and trust God based on his track record with you?

Note: Keep a journal of prayer requests and prayers that were answered. Sometimes our relationship with God is not as strong as it could be because we don't remember that God brought us through in the past. We forget, that if God had answered THAT prayer the way we wanted, we would be in trouble now. Get a journal started that chronicles your experiences with God and then go back and read your "history" together when things look rough.

CHAPTER EIGHT

Tattered Presents and Broken Gifts

I would be remiss if I didn't dedicate at least one chapter to the hole in the hearts of many women. It is that hole caused by the heartache of male/female relationships gone wrong. Most of us that are single have resigned to the fact that we will now wait on God to send us who he wants us to have. The problem is when he comes, we don't recognize him or know how to treat him. The past relationships have left us so scarred and wounded, God sends his best and we turn up our nose and hardened our hearts. We have in our mind what we want, but it may differ from what God intends to send. Yes, God's word says he will give you the desires of your heart. However if your hearts desire is God's will for your life, you need to be open to race, culture, weight, height, career choice, education, age and background. You also have to keep your past in the past. Don't let the men that have mishandled you cause you to miss your opportunity to meet your King.

I am an expert at this train of thought, having gone through it recently. I have included a copy of my journal notes, during one such bout' with my mind.

"Lord I'm in trouble, BIG trouble. You gave me what I asked for finally and I am about to blow it. I keep pushing him away like he's spoiled food. He is your gift to me and I don't know what to do with him. I am so sorry for misusing him, and perhaps hurting and losing him. As we seek to get to know each other, he pushes button, opens doors, and rips off scabs of areas that I had securely hidden away. But this man, through your spirit quickly discerns and seeks to uproot all that hinders growth and life. Pruning hurts. His bright light in my dark areas is embarrassing and confusing. Anyway, as present or gift to him ?? YUCK !! I appear tattered, ripped, worn, wounded, broken and useless.

Yet, He loves me. I know it. He proves it time and time again. He is your child and his love mimics your love for me. It's unconditional love and it is good and perfect. He gives without expecting and receives gratefully. He chips away at the stone around my heart and struggles to seek the core of who I am. My mask does not intimidate, nor fool him. My fears do not scare him and my past does not deter him. My persuasive words or evasive ways do not sway him. His goal is to simply love me and eventually build a life with me. He is not scared and he is not running. He is still here, pushing, prodding, unveiling and restoring. He gives that "I'd lay my life down for you" kind of love.

Lord, I want to learn to love like that again. When I was new and unscarred. I want to go back to the place before the divorce, before the child out of wedlock, before the first kiss, the abuse, the hurt, the bondage and the pain and love like I did when love was simple, pure and unadulterated. I want to love like it doesn't matter if they love back and my love isn't conditioned on what someone says, does or believes. I want to love the potential in others, not just where they are now. I want to be a good and perfect gift.

Everyday it's a struggle to get in your presence to confess doors I thought were closed, and reveal wounds I thought had healed. The walls I've built around my heart appear insurmountable. The masks I wear daily, aid to help even me to forget who I really am. I resist confessing what your Word says about me. It's difficult for me to even pretend to love me, yet you send me a man that loves me harder than I have ever experienced. I am afraid to love him and I am afraid to love me. This tattered, ragged present isn't a gift to anyone in its current condition. So now what do I do?

Lord, I don't want to push him away. Between you and I, I need him. You have fashioned him for me to bring healing and joy back to my life. The King you have sent to me deserves to be honored and loved like royalty. He deserves a Queen, at the very least a Princess. Create in me a clean heart or Lord and renew the right spirit in me. Show me what you see in me, show me who I am in you. Restore the innocence of my childhood, the adventure of my youth and the wisdom of my adulthood. One day, present me to your gift for me spotless, virtually virginal and ready to love him fully, more completely than he has ever experienced in his life. Give me what I need to make the vision for his life come to past. Help me bring healing in areas of his life where there is pain or darkness. I want to be a joy to him, a present he'll want forever...healed, whole and delivered !! Mold me, shape me I give my life to the Potter's hand."

I want to go over two quick things I wrote in that piece that stood out to me for the purposes of this book.

"My mask does not intimidate, nor fool him. My fears do not scare him and my past does not deter him. My persuasive words or evasive ways do not sway him. His goal is to simply love me...."

The man in your life must be mature. Not just necessarily in age, but in spirituality. He can't be a guy "playing church" if you want to get to your destiny. He has to be someone that is filled with the discerning spirit of God so he can rely on the Spirit to show him what is real about you and what is hidden behind a mask. He needs to be someone who isn't just so wrapped up in his own issues that he doesn't notice when your demeanor changes. He has to know HOW to love you. He has to care enough to put you as the priority in his life and give you the attention you need when you need it. He can't be easily swayed by what YOU say. He has to know when you are speaking out of your spirit and when you are talking out of your flesh or carnally. He has to be strong where you are weak and not be afraid to help face your fears and insecurities. He cannot be intimidated by what he sees on the surface. He must know how to dig deeper and look harder at who you really are.

Secondly, "…..his love mimics your love for me. It's unconditional love and it is good and perfect."

Ask for from God, and settle for no less than, a man that imitates

God in his love for you. Remember he can tell you ANYTHING. We as women are affected by what we hear. But, watch what he does. What he **does** indicates what he really believes and what he really feels. If he does not respect you, he will have no problem acting any kind of way around you. He has no problem disrespecting you and expecting you to not to mind. If he truly loves you as Christ loves the church, there are certain things he wouldn't, no actually couldn't do, because of his relationship with God and fear of God. No matter what you tell him, he should always stand on the Word of God. Now, that does **not** give you license to tempt a brother or put him in a position to have to wonder if you are a virtuous women. You should however, watch his character closely. If he will wildly yell obscenities at another driver, he may be impatient or a hot head and yell at you. If he will blame you for his shortcomings, he may not be a man that will take accountability and responsibility for his actions toward you or others. If he doesn't study the Word diligently now or exhort you to do it, he won't do it as your husband. Ask God to keep your eyes wide open. I prayed that prayer years ago and God has honored it every time since. I asked God, no matter what I have to see, walk in on or overhear, Don't let me be ever be fooled again. Now, I walked in on, found out and overheard some STUFF and it has not all been easy to swallow. I have been dealt some crushing blows. So if you pray that, beware-you must to be tough. But it has faithfully kept me from making very costly mistakes and from giving over the reins of my heart too soon.

 I used to say in relationships, in my naivety, that no matter **what** I would stay with "you" and work this out or that nothing would make me leave what "we" have. Like earlier, that my dear, is what my Bishop would call the "spirit of stupid". If the characteristic, the action, or the habit is severe enough to put a serious check in your spirit, get godly counsel immediately. I was at a similar crossroad in a previous relationship. I had children to think about and brutally broken heart to guard. I wanted the brother to get some help and I took steps to start that process, it was up to him from there. I personally, needed some counsel fast. As uncomfortable as it was to discuss and admit, I received the support I needed and the release from God to move on.

A Princess-Cut Diamond

Now, if you are talking about a marital relationship, that's an entirely different level and your commitment to God holds you to a higher and more serious standard. If you are a victim of spousal abuse or the lives of you and your children are at risk or not being taken care of, SEPARATE and seek God as to what to do next. An awesome example of that would be with the story of Abigail. (1 Samuel 25:3) Now the name of the man was Nabal; and the name of his wife Abigail: and she was a woman of good understanding, and of a beautiful countenance: but the man was churlish and evil in his doings; and he was of the house of Caleb. 1 Samuel tells us when, David was being pursued by Saul, and he came near to Carmel, with his troop of around six hundred men, he found himself without food, water and necessities. David sent word to Nabal, who lived nearby, that he needed food for himself and his men. Nabal declined to help. David was offended because he had previously protected Nabal's herds and shepherds. So David and around four hundred of his men went to raid Nabal's belongings and take by force what he refused to give them.

When word got to Abigail, by way of one of her husband's servants what Nabal did, she begin to immediately work at making up for Nabal foolishness. (**1 Samuel 25:18-20**) Then Abigail **made haste**, and took two hundred loaves, and two bottles of wine, and five sheep ready dressed, and five measures of parched corn, and an hundred clusters of raisins, and two hundred cakes of figs, and laid them on asses. And she said unto her servants, Go on before me; behold, I come after you. But she told not her husband Nabal. And it was so, as she rode on the ass, that she came down by the covert on the hill, and, behold, David and his men came down against her; and she met them.

(**1 Samuel 25:23-24**) And when Abigail saw David, she hasted, and lighted off the ass, and **fell before David on her face, and bowed herself to the ground**, And fell at his feet, and said, **Upon me, my lord, upon me let this iniquity be**: and let thine handmaid, I pray thee, speak in thine audience, and hear the words of thine handmaid.

Abigail was ready to stand in the gap for her husband's actions. (**1 Sam 25:25**) Let not my lord, I pray thee, **regard this man of**

Belial, even Nabal: **for as his name is, so is he; Nabal is his name**, and **folly is with him**: but I thine handmaid saw not the young men of my lord, whom thou didst send. Abigail took responsibility for him although he should have been responsible for himself. Abigail showed humility and courage.

David was satisfied and his anger subsided. He accepted Abigail's offering and sent her on home. (**1 Samuel 25:32-35**) And David said to Abigail, Blessed be the LORD God of Israel, which sent thee this day to meet me: And blessed be thy advice, and blessed be thou, which hast kept me this day from coming to shed blood, and from avenging myself with mine own hand. For in very deed, as the LORD God of Israel liveth, which hath kept me back from hurting thee, except thou hadst hasted and come to meet me, surely there had not been left unto Nabal by the morning light any that pisseth against the wall. So David received of her hand that which she had brought him, and said unto her, Go up in peace to thine house; see, I have hearkened to thy voice, and have accepted thy person.

So to my married sisters, I tell you that if you are godly you can go to God on behalf of your husband. You can sow into the king on his behalf. But understand and pay attention to the end of Abigail's story. Ten days later, God killed Nabal and David heard about it. David sent for Abigail to become his wife. Precious daughters know that God will not allow your husband to "cut the fool forever". God will change him or kill him.

Now, for men that you are getting to know and are not engaged to, DO NOT SETTLE. YOU ARE PRICELESS. YOU ARE WORTH PURSUING. Don't let any man make you feel bad about your standard. He will either step up or move on. Trust me, I've seen them come and I've seen them go. Either way Princess, you keep on walking.

Eventually, you will say like David, It was good for me that I had been afflicted. God orchestrates the yes's and the no's. If he had not yielded the disaster I was in, I would not have what I have now. But if I had not listened, cared more about what people thought or how it would "look", I may have been trapped now in a saddened state way lower than God's perfect will for me.

You have to see yourself valuable. You are not a tattered present and you do not have to receive a broken gift.

Reflection and Application

1. Look at all of your hurts in relationships that way. What did you learn? What did you do wrong? What did you do right? Where did you let him go to far? What barriers or boundaries should you have put in place?

2. Is your husband an unbeliever? Like Abigail, Go to the King on his behalf. Continue to pray for him to give his life to the Lord. Honor and serve him with all diligence, YES HIM! Regardless to what he is not, respect him as the man you want him to be. He can be won over by your lifestyle and your love for him. You are responsible for how you treat him, not for what he does to you.

3. Are you married and need a renewal? Think back to why you loved your husband in the first place. Ask the Lord to create in you a clean heart, where you can forget all the things gone wrong and receive a fresh anointing and grace to take your marriage to the next level.

4. Learn James 1:2 My brethren count it all joy when you fall into divers temptations; knowing this, that the trying of your faith worketh patience. But let patience have her perfect work, that ye may be perfect and entire wanting nothing.

CHAPTER NINE

The Unaware Advantage

As mentioned in my bio, I am a former pageant queen. The national competition was one summer in Atlanta, Georgia. When I got there and saw the competition, I tried to pick out who the most threatening competitors were. I watched for the women who were articulate, who "dressed" professionally, who were confident, who were attractive and who just seemed to "have it all together". I knew my strengths, but I didn't know theirs. I also knew my weaknesses, but I didn't know theirs. In my head, I had to rationalize, now who "looked" like the next Pageant Queen? Who could represent the crown and the pageant system in integrity? I begin working on my presentation, double checking my wardrobe, practiced my answers to common questions, reviewing the things my trainer and coaches had taught me, and rehearsed walking on the runway. I wanted to be sure that I was always at the top of my game and that I was portraying that I was a serious competitor and I came to win. I knew the other ladies were watching me as well. As the weekend developed, and we got to spend some time together, some of the ladies that I deemed as the top 10 lost points with me because of their demeanor and persona in public. There were smokers, women that cursed like sailors, some were men crazy, others wore revealing, inappropriate clothes.

What I realized was that if one of these women got in, it would not necessarily be because they were the best choice, it would be because they knew how to play the role of the best choice. Well, those people who really know me, know that I despise "the fakeness". One of my best girlfriends, Michelle, has a saying…"Don't be deep, be real". Just be who you are and let the chips fall where they may. I had to recently deal with an extremely fake person and because of how this person forcibility fits into my life and the life of my family, I have to develop a strategy to deal with the phoniness. I am still working on it. But I in turn will not be fake, this person is well aware that their demeanor is unacceptable to me.

In a competition, you make every effort to put your best foot forward. But when I saw the amazing contrast between how they acted when "the camera was rolling" versus how they really were, it was like a big act. It wasn't YOUR best foot. You were actually transforming and putting on a mask of who you needed to be to get what you wanted. The effort it took to be "two people" was just too much drama for me. It was simpler to just develop your own character to the point that you could be proud of who you really are and what you have worked to become.

Before the main evening competition, we had the private interview session. This portion was worth 50% of your score. You had to sit before the judges and answer a barrage of questions and talk about yourself and your aspirations for the crown. After this portion was over, it was time to prepare for "showtime". You put on the stage makeup, you tape this up, glue this down, push this in and pull this out…and hope for the best.

Anyway, as the competition commenced I watched other women perform before me and I got intimidated. There were singers, dancers, slide shows and I was just going to do a dramatic reading for my talent. I was good. I am dramatic in that sense, and I knew I would do well, but I still was afraid that more conventional talent would win out over what I could do. During the evening gown as I was walking out on the runway, the commentator announced my name, my education etc… and then the fact that I had five children. You heard these astonishing gasps from the audience. I couldn't tell if that was good or bad. Were they surprised that I looked so well to have five kids or were they judging me because I was a single-divorced mom with five kids? Of course, I assumed the latter and when I got back behind stage I wanted to cry. First of all I was mad that what other people thought mattered to me. I was proud to be their mom, and if the judges had any idea of what it took for me to get this far, they would be proud of me to. Secondly, I seriously thought my chances of winning had just slipped from slim to none.

I made it through the semi finals and we had gotten down to the wire and only two women were left standing. One was me and the other was announced the runner up. I had won. I really had that " I don't believe this is happening to me face' that people mimic.

After it was over, I talked to one of the ladies judging and she congratulated me and I thanked her for her support. I shared with her how nervous I was and how I was so happy that they didn't hold my talent or evening gown performances against me. She looked at me like she had no clue as to what I was talking about. She said, "Camille, I picked you after the interview, I think you actually won this pageant way before now".

A few weeks later I received copies of the judges remarks and I actually scored well in the evening gown and the talent. I got high marks for my attire and presentation, but the surprise was the comments from the interview.

" Great orator, perfect example of a Queen, would do well"

" Professional appearance, good articulation, I think we've found a number 1 contender"

"One of the only ones I liked without a run in her stocking, she was put together, she was fun and real"

I scored perfect scores all the way across. Not because I was cocky or arrogant or playing a role. I was just being me and in the words of Sally Field " They liked me, they really liked me!" Seeing that the interview was 50% of your score, unless I had just went out there later and fell on my face, I would have been tough to beat. I went into the competition with an advantage that I was unaware of.

I shared that experience to show how fear and intimidation can haunt you and cause you undue stress when you have already won the victory. Getting your life organized, facing creditors, praying over your children, resting when you should rest, stepping when you should step, believing God for the right spouse or stirring up the love and commitment for the one you have and all the other things we have talked about can be intimidating, but you already have the victory won. Your restoration back to your rightful place in the Kingdom was paid for on Calvary through Jesus blood. He also covered sickness, disease, and poverty. So, rest assured not only will God restore you to role of Princess, but you get double rewards for all the junk you had to go through to get here.

A local grocery store chain has a period of time when they honor your coupons at double the value. For example, let's say you have a coupon for 50 cents off your favorite cereal. On double coupon day, you get 50 cent off plus 50 cent more off on top of that. Hey, a dollar off cereal...that's God sent! You don't mind going through the trouble of scouring through countless newspapers and circulars. Cutting and organizing coupons isn't so much a bother when you realize you get double for your trouble. What a bargain!!

The local grocer stole his idea from God. That's right...God came up with double coupons FIRST !!! He made that deal with us years ago. remember...He said..

"Come back to the place of safety all you prisoners, for there is hope. I promise this very day that I will repay two mercies (or double KJV) for each of your woes" Zec 9:12 NLT

So..imagine for every heartache you get double joy..

For every disappointment you get double the happiness.

For every tear you get double the laughs (man, I should be cracking up...)

For every fear you get double the peace.

For lost job you get two new ones to choose from.

For every step toward poverty you get two leaps towards propserity.

For every day you went hungry you get enough back for you and enough to share.

For every destroyed marriage, you get double the years in a better one.

I could go on and on...for you see, for every ponder,

I get double the revelation!

Redeem your coupon. Take God at his word. Speak out his promises. He is watching over his word waiting to perform it.

Your new role will look weird to some. Your demeanor will be different. Your expectations will be different. Your tolerance level for ungodliness will be different. The fruit of the spirit (Love, joy, peace, longsuffering, gentleness, goodness, faith, meekness, and temperance) will be operating in your conversation, in your relationships and in your dealings with others. The things you tolerated from "him" won't wash with you anymore.

Everybody can't be in your space. I received an e-mail which stated *"The more you seek quality, respect, growth, peace of mind, love and truth around you...the easier it will become for you to decide who gets to sit in the front row and who should be moved to the balcony of Your Life "*. Beloved, I have people sitting in the parking lot of my life. I may be concerned for them and they may be on my prayer list, but they aren't going in my direction and I can't lead from the back. I have to keep on walking.

Your conduct will demand a different level of respect. Disarray and disorder frustrate you to the point that you must seek change in the situation around you. You will leave places and people better than you found them. People will wonder "Well, who does she think she is" and they will look at you strange.

As a Queen, I know what it is like to walk around with a crown on your head and have people stare at you in an awe-like state. It's a weird feeling trust me. You want to shake them and say…Hey it's just me! The reality is that the crown makes a difference. During one of my appearances, I walked into an area mall where I wasn't dressed for the appearance. I had brought my clothes to change into with me. When walking though the mall looking for the bathroom, I saw a few people and I spoke-just being polite. No one recognized who I was or even cared for that matter. They were getting their shopping done and getting a bite to eat. I entered in the bathroom, shed off my t-shirt and jeans, put on my suit, pumps and that satin sash and rhinestone crown and emerged from that bathroom as a whole new person.

When I walked out into the mall this time, I walked differently (heeled pumps will do that). I stepped like a lady, was dressed like a lady and that crown said that I was different, set apart, that there was something special about me. Every two steps, people were asking me for my autograph, and to take a picture with their child. I was approach by total strangers asking me what I won and how did I do it.

God will put people in your path to ask you what is different about you. They will want to know what you did and how you did it. Many of you will point back to this book, but ultimately I want you to point back to God. He is the restorer of your soul. He is the lifter of your head. He has crowned you in majesty and you are seated in heavenly places. He has given you beauty for ashes and for the tears you've sown you shall reap in joy.

Proclaim this now and always!

"You are an awesome spirit being with infinite potential"
"The head and not the tail"
"Above only, and not beneath"
"A Daughter of Abraham and heir to the promises of God"
"A Princess in the Kingdom of the Most High God..."

...............she saw me in the spirit in a mound of dirt. She asked God to reveal why she was seeing this and the spirit asked to her to dig in the dirt. She saw a diamond. It was dirty, grimy and muddy but a diamond nonetheless. She said that the mud, dirt was representative of the past, what I had went through, what I was believing about myself, but regardless of that in God's eyes I was still valuable. I was a diamond.

And you too are a diamond...a Princess-cut Diamond.

Reflection and Application

1. Go get yourself a Tiara...and crown yourself, "A daughter of the King!!!

Princess Points of Preparation

Regardless of what you've done, been through or look like-it does not negate the fact that because of who your daddy is, you are a joint heir to the throne.

The Word doesn't work until you do it. You will have to work the Word and watch the Word work.

Remember it is important to know the meaning of your name (who you are) and the definition of your sub-kingdom, which is your area of influence (what you are responsible for).

It may not look good, It may not feel good, But God's promise is that is must work out FOR good.

BELIEVE! Don't remember the lie that the supernatural is not possible.

Your deliverance is not just for you, but for the benefit of those who do not believe.

When Jesus yells in your tomb and tells you to "come forth" don't yell back Lord, I can't, I'm dead. Just get up and walk out.

You have the Power to Step. When it's time to go, BE OUT. You have the authority and the permission to step out of anything or away from anyone that hinders, damages or challenges your destiny.

You cannot change what has happened. But believe God to direct your path to change what happens next.

Being a Princess is as much about ministry as it is position!

Don't be a consistent pack rat. It is a sign that you believe no more is coming and it says to others this is all I have and I am getting no more. That is the sound of peasants not royalty. Be a giver.

Tell the devil, it's my house and I live here! As for me and MY house we will serve the Lord.

A Princess-Cut Diamond

Remember nanny's purse-It may look little and unassuming, but in that little tote carries the power to take an enemy out. Don't forget your weapons.

God cannot do whatever he wants to do. He must do what he said he would do. His timing and method are his to control but his promises are a contracted deal.

Encourage yourself, David did.

Relaxing isn't permanent, although a state of rest is.

Go in the strength you have.

Don't let the men that have mishandled you cause you to miss your opportunity to meet your king. Remember Abigail. The King will come back for you.

You decide who "sits" where in your life..front row or the parking lot.

Your new conduct and demeanor will command a new level of respect. Walk in your authority Princess. You are God's daughter. A daughter of the King.

Appendix

For Information on Purity with Purpose:

> Minister Loretta Cameron-Flake
> Detroit World Outreach
> 23800 W. Chicago
> Redford, MI. 48237

A Wise Women Buildeth Her House, Xulon Press
By: Minister Charisse Gibert
www.xulonpress.org

Pursuit of Purpose, Destiny Image Publishers
By: Dr. Myles Monroe

"An Awesome Spirit Being with Infinite Potential"
Quoted From: *Bishop Jack C. Wallace, Senior Pastor Detroit World Outreach*

Printed in the United States
34829LVS00005BA/145-306